THE SEARCH
FOR
FREEDOM

THE SEARCH FOR FREEDOM

FINDING FREEDOM FROM HOMOSEXUALITY

GARRETT DREW ELLIS

Pleasant Word
PW A Division of WinePress Group

Pleasant Word (a division of WinePress Publishing, PO Box 428, Enumclaw, WA 98022) functions only as book publisher. As such, the ultimate design, content, editorial accuracy, and views expressed or implied in this work are those of the author.

Unless otherwise noted, all Scriptures are taken from the *New King James Version*, © 1979, 1980, 1982 by Thomas Nelson, Inc., Publishers. Used by permission.

Scripture references marked KJV are taken from the *King James Version* of the Bible.

Scripture references marked NASB are taken from the *New American Standard Bible*, © 1960, 1962, 1963, 1968, 1971, 1972, 1973, 1975, 1977, 1995 by The Lockman Foundation. Used by permission.

Scripture references marked NLT are taken from the *Holy Bible, New Living Translation*, copyright © 1996. Used by permission of Tyndale House Publishers, Inc., Wheaton, Illinois 60189. All rights reserved.

Scripture references marked NIV are taken from the *Holy Bible, New International Version®*. NIV®. Copyright © 1973, 1978, 1984 by International Bible Society. Used by permission of Zondervan. All rights reserved.

ISBN 13: 978-1-4141-1393-7
ISBN 10: 1-4141-1393-5
Library of Congress Catalog Card Number: 2009901302

God: Every atom of my being belongs to you.
You have my love, adoration and
worship for forever and a day.

Dayona: I hope you S.H.M.I.L.Y.

CONTENTS

ACKNOWLEDGMENTS

*T*HIS BOOK COULD *not have happened without the expressed love of so many people. All of these have my sincerest love and gratitude:*

To my end all and be all, God the Father, His Son Jesus Christ and the precious Holy Spirit: I love you more than anything in this world. In you I live and move and have my being. Because you see more in me than I could ever see in myself, you have my praise, my worship, and my adoration for eternity. Plus a day.

To Dayona, God's earthly representation of His love for me: I could not have asked for a more perfect Proverbs 31 wife. Without your love, commitment, grace, and friend-ship, I would not be here today. Words cannot express how much I love you but I will try with every word I ever write. For Forever.

To Tim—my brother, my mentor, my best friend: When I was at my lowest, you came to the edge of hell to fight on my behalf. There is no one anywhere on earth like you. I love you.

To Mama Joann—This ministry is functioning largely because of your faith in God and in me. Your encouragement, your seeds, and your love kept me going when nothing else could. You have my friendship and my love forever and ever and ever…and ever.

To Pastor Louis A. Butcher Jr and the Bright Side Church family: I love you all. Thank you for your preaching, teaching, and love.

To my encouragers: Gloria Brown and Da'lynn Jordan. Thank you for your faith in me. You continually push me and my ministry forward. God bless you always.

To the staff at Pleasant Word publishing: George, Jan, Abigail and all the editors: The Christian world is blessed to have you available to publish God's inspired words. May God bless your work for many years past forever. Thank you so much.

May He grant you according to your heart's desire, and fulfill all your purpose. We will rejoice in your salvation, and in the name of our God we will set up our banners! May the LORD fulfill all your petitions.

—Psalm 20:4–5

But may the God of all grace, who called us to His eternal glory by Christ Jesus, after you have suffered a little while, perfect, establish, strengthen and settle you. To Him be the glory and dominion forever and ever. Amen.

—1 Peter 5:10–11

INTRODUCTION

WELCOME! I AM so honored to have this book in your hands! You are holding a collection of truths that I am learning to live by as I make my own journey out of a homosexual lifestyle. I wrote them all down because I have an inkling that if you have even read this far, you may be interested in how a journey like that is started and maintained.

Let me say this: I don't have all of the answers some readers may be looking for. What I do have is what God has taught me about myself and what I personally have to do to live contrary to my homosexual feelings. I believe many of the truths I have learned may be universal ones and could be helpful to you in terms of what you may be experiencing in your own life. I offer them to you in the hope that they may be of some use.

In these pages you will find Bible studies pertaining to leaving the homosexual lifestyle, as well my thoughts on what may be necessary for one to achieve the freedom so many in that lifestyle seek. Most importantly, you will find encouragement and tips for starting your own relationship and journey with God.

I do not claim to have the cure for homosexuality, and I am not a theologian or mystic; but I do have a testimony to the extreme and awesome power of God—power to change a life into something new. There was a time I thought I was alone. I thought I was the only person on earth who disliked my attraction for men. But when I found freedom in Christ, I committed myself to letting others like myself know that they are *not* alone. My desire is to walk beside you as a cheerleader for God and for your freedom. I am here to announce that *you can make it!*

This book is the result of life experience, and it is designed to be a hands-on, tangible help in your daily life. While it will help you study the Bible and figure out what the Bible says about leaving a homosexual lifestyle, more importantly, it will be a challenge to begin your own journey. I think some of the topics are necessary to confront if you want to find freedom, but they may not be as necessary for you as they were for me. That's OK. Go where God is calling you. Do what He asks you to do. I hope that if I am as transparent as possible, you can learn from my mistakes and be inspired to imitate the triumphs of many Christian men around the world.

This book is divided into topics about different aspects of the journey. Each topic has its own chapter, and in each of the chapters there are lessons on biblical themes that have helped me to find freedom. The topics follow a sequential order, but they are also designed to stand alone. Because of this, you can feel free to work on any topic for as long as you want.

In each section, I will bring you through passages of Scripture and ask you to provide answers to questions. I will encourage you to implement some spiritual disciplines in your life as you progress through the book. I do this in order for you to grow stronger in your relationship with God, because the closer you get to Him, the clearer you will see what your own journey entails.

Writing and reflection became two disciplines crucial to my own journey. Today, I can look back at some of those rants and raves I wrote down and see how God has built my character and how far He has brought me in my responses to temptation and my relationship with Christ. When I began this book, I knew I did not want to offer any kind of advice that did not include these disciplines. For this reason, there will be frequent places throughout the study marked "Personal Space." These are places for you to record feelings, thoughts, prayers—the possibilities are endless. Or, you can record these feelings in a journal or with a word processing program. Just be sure your responses are permanent and confidential, so you can look at them years later and thank God for how far you have come.

Other things I should point out:

• Practice at Scripture memorization is crucial to your freedom, and for this reason, I will frequently encourage you to memorize verses of the Bible. This is so that not only will you know what God's

XVI • THE SEARCH FOR FREEDOM

Word says, but also you will be able to digest it so it becomes a part of you, a tool to fight the enemy and temptation. The verses at the beginning of each section, as well as specially marked verses throughout, are memory verses, and they will either summarize the section or bring to light some aspect of the section. You will also find a page about Scripture cards in the appendix to help with this.

- Primarily, I will be using the New King James Version of the Bible as my chosen English translation, but any other version is perfectly sufficient to use. There are numerous search engines on the Internet offering free access to a myriad of Scripture translations and Bible study tools (see the Appendixes).

- The main purpose of this book and all its tools is to encourage your personal communication with God. Along the way I will frequently encourage you to talk to the Lord about the topic we are discussing.

- Above all else, seek the Lord! One thing is sure: you will need the Lord's direction and guidance in order to travel this road.

As we walk through this journey together, do not give up. There are going to be days where you want to throw in the towel and days you feel like you just cannot go on. There will be days when this journey seems too hard and not worth the fight. Those are the exact times to keep going, to keep moving, even if it means taking one step forward for every four steps back. It is in those times that we need to push a little harder and pray a little longer—because when we do, Christ manifests Himself and shows us He is stronger than any of our weaknesses. God said, through (and to) the apostle Paul, in 2 Corinthians 12:9, "My grace is sufficient for you, for my strength is made perfect in weakness." I will be offering tips based on what I do in times of weakness, but once again, my primary advice is going to be to seek the Lord in everything.

Take your journey seriously. Commit yourself to it because you believe your life and freedom depend on your relationship with God. The truth is: it does. The only way you are ever going to find freedom from your unwanted attractions and be empowered to live victoriously in Christ is by committing totally to seeking Him for both.

I want to hear from you, and I encourage you to log onto my Web site: *www.thesearchforfreedom.org.* The following resources are meant to accompany this study, located on the site:

- **The Iron sharpens Iron Mentorship program**: participants are able to sign up and connect with another man walking in freedom from homosexual feelings, all for the purpose of prayer, encouragement, and support.
- **A weekly discipleship email**: participants are sent a weekly email that they can use for personal Bible study and reflection.
- **Freedom Seminars**: willing participants can sponsor a seminar at their local church or ministry, where Garrett will help to educate and equip men for the journey, as well as help family members and

church leaders better minister to men leaving homosexuality.

You can send me e-mail, join the mentorship program, or ask for prayer. In addition, there are links to resources and ministries to help us all continue moving forward.

I pray for you daily. Before you even picked up this book, I was praying for you. Know that you are always on my mind. And fortunately, we have a God whose mind and heart are far bigger than my own. In Jeremiah 29:11–13, we read:

> "For I know the thoughts that I think toward you," says the Lord, "thoughts of peace and not of evil, to give you a future and a hope. Then you will call upon Me and pray to Me and I will listen to you. And you will seek Me and find Me, when you search for me with your whole heart."

I pray not only that you will begin your journey away from your unwanted feelings, but also that out of it you will see more of God, love Him more than ever, and get closer to the life He wants you to live—abundant life.

Be blessed.

Garrett Drew

CHAPTER 1

WHY I DO WHAT I DO: NOTHING BUT A WITNESS

And they overcame him by the blood of the Lamb and the word of their testimony.

—Revelation 12:11

I WANT TO TELL you who I am. Since we will be spending a lot of time together, I think you should know who is giving you all this advice and encouragement, and why I am doing it.

My name is Garrett Drew Ellis, and I am nothing more than a witness to the awesome power of God to change lives. I am not a pastor or theologian, and I am not a Bible scholar—nor am I some "fire and brimstone" preacher sent to thump you over the head with a Bible and condemn you to hell. There is something else I am not: some kind of perfect ex-homosexual. I did not write this book because I want to change every homosexual in the world. I really only wrote it for those who are unhappy and want to make changes but don't know how. I am just a simple man who was changed by God and who desires to tell the story of how He brought me through. I have no secret knowledge about the way God works or of some formula to solve one's pain. Really, I am like the blind man who was the inspiration for John Newton's famous hymn "Amazing Grace." At one point I was blind and lost, and now I can see—all because God extended me grace.

Reading the story of the blind man in the ninth chapter of John sheds some light on my identity. Here we find a man blind since birth. He was a beggar and an outcast because of his disability, and he lived on the outskirts of Jewish society. No doubt he was unhappy and confused, wondering why he was in that situation. (Sound like anyone you know? When I read it, it sounds like me!) After noticing him and his blindness, Jesus healed the man by placing some mud over his eyes and telling him to wash it off in a pool.

Now the Pharisees (the religious leaders of the day) didn't like Jesus because He claimed to be the Messiah and Savior of the world—and also because He healed this man on the Sabbath, which was the holy day of rest. So they interrogated the formerly blind man, trying to get him to say it was not Jesus who had healed him. They called Jesus a sinner incapable of healing anyone, and they wanted the man to agree to their defamation of the Christ.

Here is what the man said to the Pharisees: "He answered and said 'Whether or not He is a sinner I do not know. But one thing I do know: That though I was blind, now I see'" (John 9:25). The man did not know who Jesus really is.

He didn't have the inside scoop on religious affairs. He was simply testifying that this man called Jesus healed him from his blindness when nothing else could.

The Pharisees were enraged and hurled insults at the newly-healed man. And here is the man's profound answer: "Why this is a marvelous thing, that you do not know where He is from; yet He has opened my eyes! Now we know that God does not hear sinners, but if anyone is a worshipper of God and does His will, He hears him. Since the world began it has been unheard of that anyone opened the eyes of one who was born blind. *If this Man were not from God, He could do nothing*" (John 9:30–33, emphasis my own).

What an awesome witness! Here is a man who had never seen anything in the visible world for his entire life. Yet after being healed, he stood up to the religious leaders of the day as a witness to the God-sent authority of Jesus. All he knew was his eyes had been opened and that Jesus had opened them. He needed no more evidence than that in order to believe that God sent Jesus, whether as the Messiah or a prophet or something else.

That is also my situation. I need nothing more than the healing I have already received from Christ in order to believe and proclaim that He was sent from God for my deliverance. And going farther than that, I need nothing more to be confident that the Father sent the Son here for you, too.

The great thing is that Jesus did not leave the man there. After hearing about his interrogation at the hands of the Pharisees, Jesus went to the man and asked him if he believed He was the Son of God. When the man asked where the Son of God was so that he could believe in Him, Jesus asserted His identity as the Son Himself. And the Scripture says the man immediately confessed belief and fell at the Lord's feet in worship (John 9:35–38).

This is such an awesome testimony of what the power of belief can do. Complete confidence in the healings, blessings, and deliverances of God in our lives is all we need to build our confidence that Jesus Christ is real. We need nothing more. And when we find that confidence, it is easy to believe in and worship Jesus.

This is my story. It was easy for me to believe that Jesus is the Son of God after His freeing me from my homosexual lifestyle. It is easy for me to believe when the Lord helps me through daily temptations. And it is easy for me to tell it to you because I know that everything I am saying comes from first-hand experience and not just theory.

I am not sitting in a seat of judgment, teaching biblical principles of freedom because I think that I am better than anyone or that I have a greater hold on God. That is definitely not the case. I am still learning and digesting the principles myself. I am here because I love you and because I know from personal experience that God can release you from a homosexual tenor, just as He did for me. I am just a sinner saved by grace, nothing more. I desire nothing more than to know and be known by Him and that you might know Him also. Therefore, let us start this journey together.

Here is your first Personal Space:

Personal Space

What do you want to feel like or look like when God has set you free? What is the testimony you desire when that happens? Take some time to think about what it is you want from God, and then write it down here. I guarantee you the Lord will exceed your expectations. As the apostle Paul wrote, He "is able to do exceedingly and abundantly above all that we can ask or think" (Ephesians 3:20).

_____

_____

_____

_____

_____

_____

_____

_____

_____

_____

_____

_____

_____

_____

CHAPTER 2

STARTING THE RACE:
A RELATIONSHIP IS
NECESSARY

As the Father loved Me, I also have loved you; abide in
My love.

—John 15:9

Chapter Goals:

- To understand the nature of being relational and its
  effect on the search for freedom.
- To memorize John 15:9.

NOW, FIRST THINGS first. This journey I am
talking about is relational. It is the journey out
of homosexuality, that is true, but it is so much
more than that on a spiritual level. It's about finding the
thing that can give you freedom and then relating to that
thing as intimately as possible. It is about belonging to a
union—something very similar to what we tried to do as
practicing homosexuals—to find a lasting relationship.

We are relational beings. We all have an ingrained desire to connect with other people, with things, and with ideas outside of ourselves. That is why we come together in marriage, why we build friendships, and why we take pride in family. We are built to be connected. Even most of the things we hate about ourselves are things that spring out of a desire to be in relationship i.e. casual/anonymous sex or a use of pornography. We participate in those things because what we really want is to know ourselves better and to make sense of the world around us. All to get someone to love us. This in and of itself is not a bad thing. We were built to relate, to have our needs met, and to meet the needs of others.

The search for freedom from homosexuality is simply a search for a real relationship, something that honors God with our sexualities. Homosexuality is a search for intimacy and relationship with a person of the same sex. Relating to others of our gender is a must in life, but God simply says that we are not to do it sexually or in a marriage relationship. Since having our needs met is necessary for survival and fulfillment, it is only logical and humane to conclude that if we were to leave that attraction behind, the relationships we would be seeking to cultivate would need to be fulfilling. This was something I did not know for a long time. I thought leaving homosexuality meant that the needs I was looking to fulfill with men would go unmet. But I was wrong. Even though I knew I was committing myself to never again knowing a man sexually, I eventually learned that I could have close relationships with other men–without having to sleep with them. I even came to know, however ironic it may sound, that this journey starts with building intimacy with the person I wanted so much to know: a man.

The man of whom I am speaking happens to be Jesus Christ. All journeys begin with being intimately connected to Christ: the Christian journey, the journey out of addiction, the journey towards fulfillment and purpose, and for us, the journey out of homosexuality.

Read the words of Jesus in the tenth chapter of the gospel of John, verses nine and ten: "I am the Door. If anyone enters by Me, he will be saved, and will go in and out and find pasture...I have come that they may have life, and that they may have it more abundantly."

Except for Christianity, no other teaching, religion, philosophy, or school of thought says homosexuality can be changed. Becoming a Christian allows for this change and for many other changes. Probably the most important change of all is that we now have the ability to connect to a God who is personally involved in our welfare. Building a relationship with Jesus does not mean simply adhering to religion. It is more than that. It is about becoming close to Him, following His teachings, and becoming His friend. The Bible says that there is a "friend who sticks closer than a brother" (Proverbs 18:24), and Jesus Himself says He no longer calls us servants but rather friends (John 15:15).

This journey cannot start unless a person finds himself (or herself) in a personal relationship with Christ. Entering into a personal relationship with Christ is not something to be taken lightly or jumped into quickly. The best time to begin a relationship with God is today, but it should be an informed decision, because once again, the ability to leave an unwanted attraction is only one benefit that comes along with the relationship. There are also other considerations to take into account such as God's call for holy living, evangelism, personal character development and unending requirement of Christian love and forgiveness to those who you may not think are deserving.

I will do my best to make Christ as clear to my readers as I can in these pages, and if and when you feel you want to know Him more intimately, you can do it at that time. Many have said that the journey of a thousand miles begins with one step. I pray you will understand that for this journey that step starts with Christ.

Personal Space

Even though we will look more closely at some of these verses later, take the time to read them now, and then record your reactions.

Proverbs 8:17

_____

_____

_____

_____

John 1:12

_____

_____

_____

_____

John 14:8

_____

_____

_____

_____

John 15:4, 5, 7

_____

_____

_____

_____

Revelation 3:20

_____

_____

_____

CHAPTER 3

WHY CHRIST? WHAT'S SO SPECIAL ABOUT HIM?

Now unto Him who is able to keep you from stumbling and to present you faultless before the presence of His glory with exceeding joy, to God our Savior, who alone is wise, be glory and majesty, dominion and power, both now and forever. Amen.

—Jude 24

Chapter Goals:

- To begin to understand who Christ is and why He is qualified to be in control of our lives.
- To memorize Jude 24.

TWO OF YOUR biggest questions may be these: "Why Christ?" "Why become a Christian in order to find freedom from my same sex attractions?" The only answer I can give is this: there is no other way. I know that may sound harsh or extreme, but let me explain.

There is no other religion or school of thought I have come across that claims that homosexuality can be changed. Every person; every psychology text; every well-intentioned family member, counselor, psychologist, and friend I confided in told me that I either had to accept same-sex attraction as my lot in life or die unhappy. There was no middle ground. Christianity was the solitary voice in the world giving me any kind of hope. And eventually, I came to know that the gospel makes good on all of its claims.

Here are ten reasons why I now believe a relationship with Jesus Christ is essential to finding freedom from homosexuality—or anything else:

1. The Bible says that a relationship with Christ can be had for the taking (Luke11:9–10).
2. There were men in biblical times who left homosexuality for something better (1 Corinthians 6:9–11, especially verse 11).
3. Christ is able to grant freedom. He has the *ability* to give the freedom we are looking for (Matthew 9:28; Hebrews 2:18; Jude 24).
4. Christ wants to grant freedom. He has the *desire* to give the freedom we are looking for (2 Peter 3:9; Matthew 8:3).
5. The Lord Jesus has been given the authority and power to set captives free and liberate those in bondage (Luke 4:18–19; Isaiah 61).
6. Christ is sufficient. He is enough (2 Corinthians 12:9; Hebrews 13:8).

7. The Lord does not demand a relationship with us, but instead, He asks for it (Luke 11:9–10; Revelation 3:20).
8. Jesus Christ died for you and me, not when we were healthy and didn't need Him, but when we were unconsciously out of a relationship with Him. He loved us enough to die for us when we did not even know Him (Romans 5:6–8).
9. He loves us more than we can possibly imagine (Romans 8:38–39).
10. He did it for me: I tried other spiritual routes before becoming a Christian, but none of them worked. When I saw the claims that Christ and Christianity made and then decided to call their bluff, I was surprised to see that they fulfilled every one of them completely. It hasn't been an easy road, but it has been worth it. And I have to believe that because I was completely unworthy when He set my feet on the right path, God can do it and wants to do it for you, too.

I pray you will see Christ for who He is and that you will understand He wants and is able to be a very present help for you in your time of need.

Personal Space

Choose two or more of the above reasons for believing in Christ that speak most strongly to you. Record your thoughts, reactions, and prayers here. If you have other reasons, record those also. In addition, read the following verses that speak about who Christ is, and record your reactions to any you choose.

Luke 3:21–22; John 1, 3:16, 6:35, 14:6; Colossians 2:9–10; and Philippians 2:5–11

_____

_____

_____

_____

_____

_____

_____

_____

_____

_____

_____

_____

_____

_____

_____

_____

CHAPTER 4

LOVING CHRIST:
STARTING A RELATIONSHIP

Behold, I stand at the door and knock. If anyone hears
my voice and opens the door, I will come in to him and
dine with him, and he with Me.

—Revelation 3:20

Chapter Goals:

- To know what it takes to start a relationship with
  Christ.
- To memorize Revelation 3:20.

I T IS A pleasure to offer you the one thing in life I believe to be of any real value. Starting a relationship with
Christ is the best and most important decision you will
ever make. In it there is salvation, reconciliation with God,
everlasting life, freedom, and peace beyond anything you
can ever imagine.

But in order to enter into this personal relationship, there are a few things you need to know. The first is that no one can start your relationship with God for you. You have to do that for yourself. Here's how.

1. Believe that every man and woman on the face of this earth is, according to Scripture, separated from God because of inborn sinfulness. That includes you and me, and there is not a thing we can do in our own power to be reconciled to God because of the sin and disobedience that lie within us. This sinfulness comes from the disobedience of the first man, namely Adam, and spread to all humanity, showing itself present in the heart and actions of every human being. As the apostle Paul said in his letter to the Romans, death has spread to all men because all have sinned and fallen short of the glory of God (3:23, 5:12).

2. Believe that Jesus Christ has made it possible for us to enter into a personal relationship with Him, because He is the Son of God, God made flesh, and the express image of the invisible God (John 1; Colossians 1:15-19). God the Son makes reconciliation with God the Father possible because of three things:

   • He was born of a virgin and led a completely sinless life (Matthew 1:18–25; 2 Corinthians 15:21).

- He was beaten, disfigured, crucified, and died on a cross in order to pay for our sins against God the Father (Isaiah 53).
- He rose from the dead after three days in the tomb, conquering sin and death and granting us the privilege of access to God the Father through faith in Jesus' death, burial, and resurrection (1 Corinthians 15:3, 4; John 3:36).

3. To receive this reconciliation through Christ, you must receive Him into your life as your Lord and Savior and believe the truth about Him and His sacrifice through faith (John 1:12; Ephesians 2:8, 9).

Receiving Christ means believing these truths about Him, not just intellectually or emotionally, but mainly as an act of the *will*, by **faith**. Faith is the "substance of things hoped for, the evidence of things not seen" (Hebrews 11:1). Faith is believing in God without seeing Him, simply trusting in His Word and the working of the Holy Spirit. It is an intentional decision, not simply some spooky, mystical event. It means allowing these truths to direct your entire life while Christ rules over it as Lord and Savior.

Beyond believing these things, the only thing you need to do is repent. *Repentance* means to reconsider, to think differently. When Jesus tells us we must repent and believe in the gospel for the kingdom of God is at hand (Mark 1:15), He is telling us to think differently than we used to think and to believe the truth of the gospel. Belief and change go hand in hand.

Another meaning of the word "repent" is to change action or to turn away. To begin a personal relationship with Christ, you must be willing to change the way you have done things—to turn away from sin and to turn toward the gospel. It is never easy, but it is always possible. God will empower you to change and to believe, providing you allow Him to help you.

How does Christ do all of this once we believe and are willing to make a change? He does it through *personal invitation* (Revelation 3:20). You personally invite Christ into your life by talking to Him (prayer) and asking Him to forgive you and be your Savior. Our praying this type of prayer opens the door for Christ to enter our hearts.

I used to offer a sample prayer for people to pray to invite Christ into their hearts and lives. But I have learned that because your relationship with Him is purely personal, no one can really tell you what to pray. You have to do so for yourself. But as a piece of advice, use the truths stated here as guidelines and look to Romans 10:9–10 as a starting point. Seal what you pray with the words "in Jesus' name." It is your belief in His name and what He has done for you that will get your prayer answered (Rom 10:9).

If you are ready and willing, you can take the time to pray that prayer now. If you feel led to do so, write out your prayer of confession, belief, and repentance, so that years down the road you can read the words that started you on your journey.

_____

_____

_____

_____

_____

_____

_____

_____

_____

_____

If you have prayed a prayer of confession and invitation, granting Christ control of your life, you can be assured that He has come(Rom 10:9).

BUT HOW DO YOU KNOW FOR SURE?

Your assurance can rest in this: He promised. We can know that Christ has entered our lives and taken control of them because He promised He would. And His presence can be evidenced by both a desire to do the will of God and a hope in the power of Christ that is so strong you feel able to conquer all of the strongholds in life, *moment* by *moment*.

Philippians 2:12–13 says to "work out your salvation with fear and trembling, for it is God who is at work in you." Any relationship has to be cultivated and strengthened in order to reap its benefits. The same thing is true of our relationship with Christ. The Lord promised to come into our lives, so now we have to live like He is there.

These things and more happened when you invited Christ in:

- You were forgiven for every sin or wrong you have ever committed. The price of Christ's blood (shed in His death) is enough payment in the eyes of the Father for your sin (Colossians 1:13–14).
- You received eternal life. Everyone has to die a physical death, but now you can be assured that you will obtain heaven afterwards (John 3:16–17, 5:24).
- You became a child of God (John 1:12).
- The Holy Spirit entered you and will empower you to be able to make right choices (John 14:16–17, 16:13).

Be assured of these things, and walk in the newness of life (Romans 6:4). Stand fast in the liberty with which Christ has set you free (Galatians 5:1).

SUGGESTIONS FOR MOVING FORWARD

- Pray daily. Ask God for the power to overcome temptation moment by moment.
- Continue with the studies and devotionals in this book. The main purpose of our journey together is to become closer in our relationship to Christ so we can know Him better and leave behind the sexual sins we do not want to commit.
- Tell someone about your new decision, perhaps find a Christian who can help you stay accountable and mentor you. (I can offer assistance in this area.)
- Find a good Bible-believing church, where Christ is honored and His Word is preached accurately. Do not

wait, take the initiative to call or find one. (Again, I can help if needed.)

- *Contact me.* I will rejoice with you; pray with you; and make sure you receive some Bible literature, a Scripture reading plan, and a Bible, if you need one.
- Thank God daily through prayer and praise for His presence in your life. We serve a God who loves to know that we love Him.

Personal Space

Record your thoughts and reactions to this section. If you started a relationship with Christ today, write out a testimony.

_____

_____

_____

_____

_____

_____

_____

_____

_____

God bless you! I pray for the best of God's will in your life. Let's journey on together.

CHAPTER 5

THE THINGS
WE MUST BELIEVE

Do you not know that the unrighteous will not inherit the
kingdom of God? Do not be deceived. Neither fornicators, nor idolaters, nor adulterers, nor homosexuals, nor
sodomites, nor thieves, nor covetous, nor drunkards,
nor revilers, nor extortioners will inherit the kingdom
of God.

—1 Corinthians 6:9–10

For God did not send His Son into the world to condemn
the world, but that the world through Him might be
saved.

—John 3:17

Chapter Goals:

- To understand that certain truths must be acknowledged in order to walk the journey of freedom.
- To memorize 1 Corinthians 6:9–10 and John 3:17.

I N THIS CHAPTER I must discuss a very hard and extremely sensitive subject. I have dreaded writing this chapter, because in my journey, it is probably the hardest pill I have had to swallow. But it is a necessary.

I have said before that my goal is not to debate the morality of homosexuality. I am not a pastor or theologian or Christian thought-leader; I am simply presenting a way of escape for men who want one. That way of escape means accepting as truth the standards God has set. Some of the truths are obvious ones, but others are not so obvious. I ask that you open your heart and be willing to learn as we take the time to evaluate our stance on each one.

1. In God's eyes, homosexuality is sin. There is no getting around it. There is much debate going on in today's world about the Scripture and its teaching on homosexuality. But in my eyes, the Word of God is clear as to what a healthy, God-fearing sexuality should look like. I say this not as a man looking from the outside in, for I have come to accept this as truth even though my emotions and physical desires have felt otherwise. I felt sexually attracted to other men, even though I did not want to feel that way. I was hearing I was in a place of sin for this attraction, and this put me on the defense. It has done the same to many others. Yet, regardless of how we feel, the Bible is clear that homosexuality is sin. Either we accept it or not. Following are some Scriptures that reveal God's stance toward homosexuality:

Old Testament

- Genesis 19:1–7 is the story of the destruction of Sodom and Gomorrah, part of which may have been due to homosexual activity. Although I do not know if this was the sole reason for the destruction, I think it is obvious it was at least one of the reasons.

- Leviticus 18:22 is part of the Old Testament law that seems to have forbidden homosexual acts.
- Leviticus 20:13 is a continuation of the law forbidding homosexual acts.
- Judges 19:21–23 is another account of homosexual acts and their prohibition.

New Testament

- Romans 1:24–32 is Paul's explanation regarding the immorality of homosexuality, and other acts, and the position of fellowship those who practice such acts forfeit with God.
- In 1 Corinthians 6:9–10, Paul states that people who continually practice immorality in the eyes of God are not going to find a place in the kingdom. (In verse 11 we find the basis for believing that even men in the ancient church were walking in freedom from homosexuality.)

As I have said before, there is much debate over the historicity and original meaning of these and other verses. But my own reading of Scripture and my own experience with homosexuality convince me that these verses mean exactly what they say. Even if some argue that certain verses do not prohibit homosexuality, it is clear from a biblical stance on a healthy sexuality in general (Genesis 2–4) that same-sex relationships are the opposite of what God intended for His creation.

Each of us must decide individually what our position is regarding these and other Scriptures that express disapproval of sexual immorality and lust. My friend, if you believe them to be untrue or untrustworthy, there is hardly any reason to wrestle with the principles presented in this book, because the rest of the principles here are founded on the view that the Bible is true and trustworthy. But if you can either accept them as truth or are open to additional reflection before making an informed decision, I encourage you to continue reading. The rest of this book will benefit you immensely.

I want to clarify something. I did not choose to walk away from homosexuality solely because Scripture convinced me it was wrong. That was certainly part of the reason, but another part was that my experience as a practicing homosexual did not offer evidence otherwise. I was unhappy and unfulfilled, and I could not find peace. Even in homosexual monogamy, I could not find joy or contentment or a sense of fellowship with my Creator. For me, homosexuality was a bad trip down a very bumpy road, and even when I gave relationship-building an honest chance, it did nothing to convince me real contentment was in reach.

We each have to decide where to stand. Does our allegiance lie with the God of the Bible and the Creator of the universe? If it does, I see no way around forsaking the practice of homosexuality. If it does not, there is the chance to see homosexual acts through God's eyes and to come to

Him for help. (As a side note, I will say that I do not think that this is a decision we need to make for society as a whole. It is one that is based upon Christian conviction or empathy, a totally personal and individual stance.)

Personal Space

Where are you with this foundational decision? Take this space to evaluate your heart and your feelings. Are you committed to these truths? If not, can you make the effort to engage in open-minded, truth-seeking research?

_____

_____

_____

_____

_____

_____

_____

_____

_____

_____

_____

_____

_____

_____

_____

_____

_____

_____

_____

_____

_____

Certain truths need to be acknowledged to walk the road to freedom. The truth about homosexuality is only one of them. You also have to accept the fact that freedom is possible. Some people will tell you that if you are a homosexual, God is against you and change in any event is not possible. And I admit that there have been times I felt that the homosexual attraction is so strong, so ingrained in my very being, that it seems it could never be changed. But this is not true. The gospel of John says, "For God did not send His Son into the world to condemn the world, but that the world through Him might be saved" (3:17).

Christ is not against us. He is against the acts we commit, but He is not against *us*. It is the same as if He were a parent whose son was on drugs. A parent in that situation hates what his (or her) child does, but does not hate the child. A parent's love is still constant. We have to hang onto the truth that nothing can separate us from God's love (Romans 8:38–39). We can be separated from His fellowship, but never from His love.

Here is what the apostle Paul said in 1 Corinthians 6:9–11: "Do you not know that the unrighteous will not inherit the kingdom of God? Do not be deceived. Neither fornicators, nor idolaters, nor adulterers, nor homosexuals, nor sodomites, nor thieves, nor covetous, nor drunkards, nor revilers, nor extortioners will inherit the kingdom of God. And such were some of you. But you were washed, but you were sanctified, but you were justified in the name of the Lord Jesus and by the Spirit of our God."

What does the verse say? "Such *were* some of you" (emphasis mine). This verse is telling us that even in the ancient church, men were being released from homosexuality. They were being washed, sanctified (purified), and justified (absolved) by God. Regardless of what the media makes it look like, men have been consistently overcoming homosexuality for thousands of years. When you have a moment, visit www. exodus-intenational.org and read some of the overcoming testimonies of men from all across the world.

We can be changed. What that change actually looks like might not be what we expect it to look like, but we don't have to sit around locked between hating homosexuality and thinking change is impossible.

In Luke 4:18, Christ gives us a glimpse into one of the reasons He came to the earth: "The Spirit of the LORD is upon Me, because He has anointed Me to preach the gospel to the poor; He has sent Me to heal the brokenhearted, to proclaim liberty to the captives and recovery of sight to the blind, to set at liberty those who are oppressed; to proclaim the acceptable year of the LORD." In other words, *He came to set us free!* Jesus' sole reason for walking the earth was so that through His earthly ministry, His death on the cross, and His resurrection from the grave we could find fellowship with the Father and liberty and salvation from sin. "Therefore if the Son makes you free, you shall be free indeed" (John 8:36).

Don't accept condemnation. It will stop you from walking in freedom, because it says that you are not worthy, that you have made mistakes, that you are any one of the filthy, disgusting words the world has given homosexuals. I have come shockingly close to giving up numerous times because I felt condemned. But I remind myself every day that Jesus Christ came not only to show the truth of God's Word and to set me free, but also He came to extend *grace*. John 1:7 says that "this man came for a witness, to bear witness of the Light, that all through him might believe."

The Word, Jesus Christ (see John 1), was full of both grace and truth. He did not rail against homosexuality but extended grace; He gave a hand up. I imagine the Lord saying, "My people need to hear the truth. But they also need my grace to walk in the truth. If I don't extend it to them, they may never find it." Apart from grace, the truth has no power. Anyone who beats you down and makes you feel like less of a human because you practiced homosexuality—or because you don't want to practice it anymore—does not know the grace of God and is not speaking the truth in love.

Personal Space

Stop and reflect on these truths. Take the time to evaluate them, to journal about them, to pray about them, and to bring your raw emotions before God. Accepting these truths can hurt, but going to God in sincerity and complete transparency is the way to find grace to make it through.

_____

_____

_____

_____

_____

_____

_____

_____

_____

_____

_____

_____

_____

_____

_____

_____

_____

_____

_____

_____

CHAPTER 6

FREEDOM: WALKING
IN THE NEWNESS OF LIFE

Now the Lord is the Spirit, and where the Spirit of the
Lord is, there is liberty.

—2 Corinthians 3:17

Chapter Goals:

- To understand what freedom in Christ looks like in relation to healing from homosexuality.
- To understand and be able to implement the three aspects of biblical freedom: truth, choice, and relationship.
- To memorize 2 Corinthians 3:17.

GOD WANTS US to live life in freedom. Yet we know that the lives of lust, promiscuity, and unnatural affections that many of us have led are anything but liberating. To find freedom from homosexuality, we need to know what freedom from homosexuality actually is, as well as what it is not. In this chapter we will look at the definition of biblical freedom and its effect on homosexuality. We will also define truth, choice, and relationship, the three main components that make up biblical freedom.

FREE/FREEDOM/LIBERTY

In the Bible, the term "to free" is defined in the Greek as "to deliver or liberate." "Liberty" is defined as "being unrestrained or free to go on no longer as a slave." This is the context for the word "liberty" used in 2 Corinthians 3:17, when Paul states, "Where the Spirit of the Lord is, there is liberty."

The *American Heritage Dictionary* defines "freedom" as: 1) the condition of being free of restraints, 2) liberty of a person from slavery, oppression or incarceration, and 3) the capacity to exercise choice or free will.

In my own journey, this is what I have found freedom to be: *freedom is the ability to choose how I will respond in any given situation without being negatively influenced by either internal or external forces.* I believe my definition is in line with biblical truth. I have personally experienced this kind of freedom since committing myself to Christ and allowing Him to direct my sexuality. I feel unrestrained and not at all like a slave to a lifestyle that I hated. I feel liberated from a life that seemed very much like incarceration.

Now let's look at the three essential aspects of getting free and staying free.

THE THREE COMPONENTS OF BIBLICAL FREEDOM

1. Truth

I have found that it is crucial for us to accept the truth of God's Word in its entirety. We have to learn to tailor ourselves to His Word, not the other way around. Only then will we be free.

Again, there is no point in pursuing biblical freedom if you do not believe what the Bible says about truth. John 8:32, 36 states: "And you shall know the truth, and the truth shall make you free....Therefore if the Son makes you free, you shall be free indeed."

Use the Scripture above to fill in the missing blanks.

"And you shall know the _____ and the _____ shall make you free...."

There are two aspects to the word "truth" that we need to understand.

- *Who* is the truth? (John 14:6) _____
  _____

  That's right. Jesus is the truth.
- *What* is the truth? (Read 2 Timothy 3:16; John 5:39; Mark 13:31; John 8:38–51.) _____
  _____

We need to understand that Jesus is *the Truth*. His testimony, His witness, every word that proceeds forth out of His mouth, and every word of the Bible is *the Truth*. It is *reality*—not some made up mythology.

This includes what the Bible says about homosexuality. I know that it may be hard to accept, especially when our feelings for men seem to be so natural. But what the Bible has to say about it not being acceptable in God's eyes is the truth. For us who are seeking a way out, it may seem understandable. But for some, it is not. But they are not seeking a way out. *You* are. And if you are going to find freedom, you have to accept this. (Refer back to the section entitled "The Things We Must Believe.")

2. *Choice*

The second principle that I have come to find plays a part in our freedom is *choice*. I do not have the answer to the debate about predestination, but in regards to freedom, I hope to help you answer this question: Are we agents working under our own free will, or are we puppets on some stage?

Joshua 25:15 says, "And if it seems evil to you to serve the LORD, choose for yourselves this day whom you will serve, whether the gods which your fathers served that were on the other side of the River, or the gods of the Amorites, in whose land you dwell. But as for me and my house, we will serve the LORD."

What is Joshua asking the children of Israel to do?

_____

_____

_____

God deals with us by granting us free will and choice. At no point in time do we find God making anyone do anything. He gives options, such as those we see in these verses. He knows that in the light of eternity there are really only two options—life or death. Even though He won't force anything on us, He does promise to do things for us in return for our affection (life) and to be absent from our decisions if we don't love Him (death). This concept is called a *covenant*.

The dictionary defines "covenant" as "an agreement, pact or contract." For our purposes, we will not go into the different covenants that God has instituted, except for the current one, the "new covenant" that Christ started with the eating of the Passover meal and implemented with His death on the cross (Luke 22:20). The new covenant promises that if we choose to believe in Christ and the price of death He paid for our sins, we will be saved from destruction and God's wrath as well as be given power to live victoriously (see Romans 10:8–10). This age of the new covenant is often called "the church age" or "the age of grace."

More than anything, my journey towards freedom from homosexual behavior has been empowered by the increased ability to come to God willingly. When I began to see that He would not force me but would instead ask me to love Him and repent from homosexuality, I found I could choose how to respond in situations rather than feeling addicted to or compelled to do things I didn't want to do. Our compulsions don't have to be so. We are empowered by God to make choices for ourselves. We do not have to bow at the feet of some outside, negative force.

Personal Space

Do you feel like you are empowered to make your own choice in regards to your freedom? If not, pray and ask God to show you how to see and do this.

_____

_____

_____

_____

_____

I began to look at my healing as a choice after I found this truth in the book of Deuteronomy 30:19–20. Moses says to the people, "I call heaven and earth to witness against you today, that I have set before you life and death, the blessing and the curse. So choose life in order that you may live, you and your descendants, by loving the Lord your God, by obeying His voice and by holding fast to Him; for this is your life and the length of your days ..."

What is he asking the people to do?

_____

What is he giving them?

_____

In this passage we see Moses offering the people choices that are polar opposites: life vs. death, blessing vs. cursing. And immediately after he lists the options, he encourages them to choose God, pointing them to the resources they need to do just that.

God was the source of Moses' authority, and through Moses, God presented right and wrong, left and right, and then let the people make the choice, even though His desire was for them to live and be free. God doesn't force anything. This is one of the main things that I love about God, one of the main reasons that I opted for giving Him a chance.

Let's look at an example where this model is repeated. Read Matthew 7:13–14. What significance do you see in the fact that Jesus says there are 2 different roads?

_____

_____

Again, we see two paths. We see a presentation of two different ways of living, along with a request to choose the way that leads to life. Jesus is presenting the choices the same way Moses did—with a desire for you to choose the right path, while still giving you the right to make your own choice. This is what I think freedom is. It's the ability to choose life, coupled with God giving us the right and the resources to do so.

Personal Space

Do you feel like you have the resources to choose life over death? Purity over promiscuity? To choose between men and what God wants for your life? Can you believe that God is giving you a choice while wanting you to succeed?

_____

_____

_____

_____

_____

_____

_____

_____

Now, in the world of the "ex-gay movement," you will sometimes hear teachers say true freedom and healing will look like a complete change in desire and a loss of taste for any kind of homosexual contact. Some report miraculous and divine healings. I am not here to discredit these teachings. I believe in a God who can perform miracles, who can instantly take away cravings, desires, and obsessions. I am not going to tell you not to petition God for a miracle. But I will say that I do not think that this is the norm and that you have to be prepared for God to say either "yes" or "no." I think that it would be foolish to limit God and say that He hasn't granted you freedom if it does not look like the complete change described above.

So, in this book, when I say that I have been healed or set free, what I am saying is that I have been empowered by God to live by my definition of freedom:

Freedom is the ability to *choose* how I will respond in any given situation without being negatively influenced by either internal or external forces.

That doesn't mean that I will never again experience a desire to be with a man. It means that I no longer feel obligated to do so. I have learned other positive, God-pleasing ways to fulfill my need for same-sex intimacy.

I say that it would be foolish to limit God to a legalistic view of freedom because such a large part of Scripture is devoted to making choices and learning to exercise the fruit of the Spirit. God will intervene to give us power make choices not to sin and to fight and be victorious over our sinful nature but I don't think that He always erases the problem completely. Let's see what He says about this.

What is the fruit of the Spirit? What is the last characteristic in the list? Look at Galatians 5:22–23 and make a list of the different qualities:

_____

_____

_____

The Greek word for "temperance" or "self-control" is *egkrateia,* which means to have control of one's emotions, desires, and actions by one's own will.

One's own will. Pay close attention to this part of the definition. Self-control not only includes reining in one's desires, but also means one is doing so by *an act of the will.* It's not really self-control if some force outside of you wipes away the problem or solves the problem for you. You have to do it, and you have to want to do it. And more than just wanting to, you have to *make* yourself do it.

Look at 1 Corinthians 9:27. What is Paul saying that he does to his body? Why?

_____

_____

_____

Paul is saying that he has a purpose, namely to preach and have that preaching be effective. So he disciplines himself to be able to fulfill this purpose. He places his body, flesh, and will under such control that they have no choice but to do his bidding. In that same spirit, you and I have a purpose in mind—to live in freedom from and not in bondage to sexual sin. Are we any different than Paul? Do we not need to discipline ourselves?

Let's look at some more verses. Record how the fruit of self-control plays a part in each of the verses:

Choose life in order that you may live ... (Deuteronomy 30:19, emphasis mine)

_____

_____

_____

_____

It was for freedom that Christ set us free; therefore keep *standing firm* and do not be subject again to a yoke of slavery. (Galatians 5:1, emphasis mine)

_____

_____

_____

_____

Do you not know that those who run in a race all run, but one receives the prize? *Run in such a way that you may obtain it.* (1 Corinthians 9:24, emphasis mine)

_____

_____

_____

_____

No temptation has overtaken you except that which is common to man; but God is faithful, who will not allow you to be tempted beyond what you are able, *but with the temptation will also make the way of escape*, that you may be able to bear it. (1 Corinthians 1:13, emphasis mine)

_____

_____

_____

_____

Concerning this thing I pleaded with the Lord three times that it might depart from me. And He said, "My grace is sufficient for you, for My strength is made perfect in weakness." Therefore most gladly I will rather boast in my infirmities, that the power of Christ may rest upon me . . . . For when I am weak, then I am strong. (2 Corinthians 2:8–10)

_____

_____

_____

_____

Blessed is the man who *endures* temptation ... (James 1:12, emphasis mine)

_____

_____

_____

_____

But he who looks into the perfect law of liberty and *continues in it,* and is not a forgetful hearer but a doer of the work, this one will be blessed in what he does. (James 1:25, emphasis mine)

_____

_____

_____

_____

Indeed we count them blessed who *endure*. You have heard
of the perseverance of Job and seen the end intended by the
Lord—that the Lord is very compassionate and merciful.
(James 5:11, emphasis mine)

_____

_____

_____

_____

I think these verses make it clear that freedom, life, and
liberty come as an act of the will. You have to *choose* to live.
You have to make a conscious effort to live and remain in
a state of control. God will empower you to do so, but it's
still your choice to live or not.

3. *Relationship*

When it all comes down to it, our relationship with
Christ is what is going to bring us through. We have spent
a lot of time talking about a relationship with Christ, but I
think it is good to look at it again. We have to know Him
intimately and be in a place of fellowship with Him not only
in order to be granted freedom, but also in order to *remain*
free. Everything always goes back to where we are in our
relationship with Him.

Read John 15:1–16. What does Jesus tell us to do in verses 4 and 5? What do you think He means?

_____

_____

_____

The word "abide" in the Greek is *meno*, and it means to "stay (in a given place, state, relation, or expectancy), to abide, continue, dwell, endure, be present, remain, stand or tarry for."

The picture that Jesus gives us in John 15 is of a tree, where He is the "true vine," the Father is the "Husbandman" or gardener, and we are the branches connected to the vine. The Father prunes and tends the tree, and we, the branches, need to stay connected to the trunk so that we can "bear fruit."

Staying connected to Jesus means staying in the Word of God, staying connected through prayer, responding to the leading of the Holy Spirit, and remaining under the lordship of Christ. He is the trunk of my tree. If I am going to blossom, I have to stay connected to the tree.

You have to believe this! I know that it seems like a lot of faith is necessary to believe the Bible and the truth about Christ, but I can testify that if you hang in there and keep the faith, you can abide! You can stay connected!

Read verses five and six. Besides abiding, what is Jesus expecting us to do?

_____

_____

_____

He is expecting us to bear fruit. What does bearing
fruit mean to you?

_____

_____

_____

What happens if we don't? (See verse 6—also look at
verses 1 and 2.)

_____

_____

_____

For us, bearing fruit will be our maintaining a godly
sexuality. It will mean not sinning against our bodies. It
will mean fleeing sexual immorality. Why? Because our
bodies and our sexuality belong to the Lord (1 Corinthians
6:13–20).

If we don't bear fruit, we are not being productive, not
staying connected. And anything that is not productive is
useless, unless it is made better (verses 5 and 6). We also
will never find satisfaction or freedom. Staying connected,
abiding, and bearing fruit are crucial if we expect to find
freedom in Christ.

The New International Version of the Bible makes clear a
good point in verses 1 and 2. Let's look Jesus' words in this

version: "I am the true vine and my Father is the gardener. He cuts off every branch in me that bears no fruit, while every branch that does bear fruit He prunes so that it will be even more fruitful."

> With reference to His asking us to abide in Christ, what does God say He will do to the branches that *do* bear fruit?

_____

_____

> Why?

_____

_____

_____

Most gardeners will tell you that pruning plants is essential if they are ever going to grow and produce even more fruit and blossoms that exceed the previous blossoms in beauty and production. We need to accept that temptation is from the enemy and entices us to sin. But tests and trials (pruning) come from God in the hopes that we *pass* the test and increase in the development of our character (James 1:2-4). Be encouraged! They are not there to harm you but to prune you.

The question you are probably asking is, "How do I do this?" Read verses 7–11. Christ is giving us something to put on the inside of us to help us abide and bear fruit. What is it? _____

Psalm 119 is known for its high praises of God's Word. It continuously repeats things about God's Word, commandments, testimonies, statutes, precepts, law, judgments, and ways, and it couples everything with praise, adoration, meditation, undying hope, and love for the Word of God. The writer is deeply in love with God's Word and teachings, realizing that in them he will find life and direction.

It should be the same with us. In verses 7–11 of John 15, Jesus tells us that if we love Him, we will keep His words in us. The writer in Psalm 119:11 tells the Lord, "Your word have I hidden in my heart, that I might not sin against you." This verse reiterates the point that we have to align ourselves to God's Word and truth. Jesus is showing us that our relationship with Him and the Father depends on our doing so. His words and teachings have to be on the inside of us, a part of us, so much so that we are unable to separate ourselves from what He wants for us.

In John 15:15, we finally come to what a relationship is all about: *intimacy*. Jesus calls us something in this verse. What is it? _____

We mean more to Him than just servants. He is God Himself; He can make us serve Him if He wants to, but He doesn't. He calls us something more intimate. He calls us His *friends*.

How cool is that?

Jesus goes on to say that when we stay connected to Him through obeying His commandments and the things that He asks of us, we are granted intimate relationship with Him and have the right to ask Him to do for us the things we need Him to do (verse 16). So, maintain your relationship with Him through obedience and fellowship, and He will grant you the freedom you ask for. He just promised it!

God does not desire robots. Let me make a point in all caps so that you get my meaning:

YOUR FREEDOM IS TIED UP IN YOUR DEDICATION TO GOD AND YOUR DISCIPLINE OF YOUR FLESH.

- God wants you to choose to love Him. Like any human father, He does not want us to walk through life sheltered, pampered, and babied, simply because He knows we will appreciate Him and our lives more when we can overcome those things that hold us back.
- God wants you to know the truth about Him, to know who He is and what He says.
- God wants you to abide, to remain rooted in Him and His truth. Live like you want to honor Him. Live like He is standing next to you. Live like you love Him.
- God wants you close to Him. Stay as close to God as you possibly can. Treat Him the same way you would treat a lover. Dote on Him, love Him, and show Him that you are His. This will put you in a place of intimacy, an intimacy that we looked for in the men around us. It's not always easy, but it is always possible. You will make mistakes sometimes but you can always reconnect yourself to the Vine.

Freedom. It can be yours!

Personal Space

Have a conversation with God about what you desire from Him. Talk to Him honestly about your feelings on the topic of freedom. What does it mean to you? Are you committed to pursuing it?

_____

_____

_____

_____

_____

_____

_____

_____

_____

_____

_____

_____

_____

_____

_____

_____

_____

CHAPTER 7

TEMPTATION

PART 1

Be sober, be vigilant; because your adversary the devil walks about like a roaring lion, seeking whom he may devour. Resist him, steadfast in the faith, knowing that the same sufferings are experienced by your brotherhood in the world.

—1 Peter 5:8–9

Section Goals:

- To understand the nature of temptation—what it is and what it is not.
- To understand the two aspects of temptation.
- To memorize 1 Peter 5:8–9.

TEMPTATION IS VERY real and is one of the biggest obstacles that stands between us and sexual purity. It is lurking behind every corner, in every doorway, and in every shadow. It desires to take your life, snuff you out, and then laugh at you as you fall beneath its powerful, death-like grip.

Not to scare you or anything. But I really need you to recognize the seriousness of this situation. If you are going to overcome temptations when they come your way, you have to know what you're dealing with and how to handle them.

The word "tempt" is defined as 1) to entice someone to commit an unwise or immoral act, especially by promise or reward; 2) to be inviting or attractive to; 3) To provoke or risk provoking.

A temptation is something that *tempts* or *entices*. Both of these words have negative connotations, meaning that they are often used when speaking about an allurement to do wrong or evil. They are very close to other words in the Bible that are similar in meaning but that hold different connotations. These words include "test," "trial," and "tried." (More on the differences among these words later.)

You will see that in the Bible, temptation always holds a negative connotation and is always referring to something that is trying to get you to do wrong or go against what God is telling you to do.

Can you think of any temptations in your life now? I can think of a lot in mine. Porn stores, especially those with private booths, are a big one. Chat rooms and Web pages are others. It is good to know what it is that tempts you so that you can do your best to fight it off.

Personal Space

Take an inventory of the things that tempt you. What things have the potential to get you to do wrong? These things can be sexual and non-sexual. List them here. Be precise and detailed—we will refer to this list later on.

_____

_____

_____

_____

_____

_____

_____

_____

_____

_____

_____

_____

_____

One thing that we need to understand is that these temptations, these enticements to sin, do not just come out of thin air. They aren't arbitrary. They have two very real forces behind them. The first force is the most obvious, but the second may not be so obvious.

Brother, the first force is the enemy—his name is Satan. He goes by the names Lucifer, Beelzebub, the devil, and the Prince of Darkness. Do not think of him as the modern day depiction of him—i.e. the red man with the pitchfork and horns—he is much more than that. Think of him as the force behind everything that is in opposition to God. Think of the embodiment of evil, the exact opposite of God in regards to personality. He is nowhere near as powerful as God, but he does have power.

Let's go to Scripture. Read Ephesians 6:11–12. In verse 11, what and who does it say we are standing against?

The_____ of the _____.

The King James Version says the "wiles" of the devil. Other translations use the words "schemes," "strategies," or "tricks." What it boils down to is that we are standing against the devil and all of the strategies he can cook up for tempting us and making us disobey God. This means that you can look at all the items on your list of personal temptations as tools that our enemy uses and throws your way. When you can see them as such, it is easier to hate them when they seem so appealing.

Let's go on to verse 12. It reads, "For we wrestle not against flesh and blood, but against principalities, against powers, against the rulers of the darkness of this world, against spiritual wickedness in high places." This verse reiterates the fact that there is a system of darkness, of evil that is present in this world, with the devil being head demon, if you will. Now I am not a person who is superstitious or into a lot of mysticism. But I do believe what the Bible says in this verse. We are fighting against a very strong power of evil, and we need to be aware that it is there and active so we can actively fight it.

Now let's look at the first memory verse of this section. Read 1 Peter 5:8–9 again:

Stay alert! Watch out for your great enemy, the devil. He prowls around like a roaring lion, looking for someone to devour.[9] Stand firm against him, and be strong in your faith. Remember that your Christian brothers and sisters[a] all over the world are going through the same kind of suffering you are.

—NLT

Now take a look at John 10:10:

The thief does not come except to steal and to kill and to destroy. But I [Jesus] come that they may have life, and that they may have it more abundantly.

Personal Space

Are you committed to resisting the enemy? Even if you don't yet know how to fight him, are you committed to learning? Write some thoughts here.

_____

_____

_____

_____

_____

When we began this discussion, I said that there were two forces at work in this world that bring temptation and that the second might not be so obvious. Want to know what the other one is?

It's you.

In the book of Romans, Paul talks about a war that is going on inside of him. He speaks of two natures, two adversaries, both fighting for dominance over his actions. The New Living Translation gives a very clear, modern rendering of his words:

> I don't understand myself at all, for I really want to do what is right, but I don't do it. Instead I do the very thing I hate. I know perfectly well that what I am doing is wrong, and my bad conscience shows that I agree that the law is good. But I can't help myself, because it is sin inside me that makes me do these evil things.
>
> I know I am rotten through and through so far as my old sinful nature is concerned. *No matter which way I turn, I can't make myself do right. I want to, but I can't. When I want to do good, I don't. And when I try not to do wrong, I do it anyway.* But if I am doing what I don't want to do, I am not really the one doing it; the sin within me is doing it.
>
> It seems to be a fact of life that when I want to do what is right, I inevitably do what is wrong. I love God's

law with all my heart. *But there is another law at work within me that is at war with my mind.* This law wins the fight and makes me a slave to the sin that is still within me. Oh, what a miserable person I am! Who will free me from this life that is dominated by sin? Thank God! The answer is in Jesus Christ our Lord. So you see how it is: In my mind I really want to obey God's law but because of my sinful nature I am a slave to sin.

—Romans 8:15–25, italics mine

There is a law at work in us that wants us to do the very things that are contrary to the things of God. It is our sin nature, the sin nature that infected all of mankind at the fall of man. It is a nature that desires to see us die in our sins, totally separated from God. Consider Romans 5:12 (NLT): "When Adam sinned, sin entered the entire human race. Adam's sin brought death, so death spread to everyone, for everyone sinned." Because of one man, we all have to deal with the sin nature being present in our lives.

We all do things that we don't want to do. Something inside of me pushed me to sleep with men when my body said "yes" but my heart said "no." Even when I was still in bondage during my marriage, when I wanted to do right, I couldn't, because something was compelling me in the opposite direction. I don't doubt that you have felt the same way.

Personal Space

Do you feel this way? Can you see the contrast between the things you want to do and the things you are compelled to do?

_____

_____

_____

_____

_____

_____

This is not meant to scare you, condemn you, or give you a license to sin. It is meant to encourage you and to help you understand that there is a part of every human alive that compels him or her to do things that are opposite of God's will. There is a way to fight against this "dark side." But before we look at how to do that, let's talk about temptation some more.

Personal Space

Have you ever felt alone? Have you ever felt that no one understands what it feels like to hate being sexually attracted to another man? If so, why do you think that is?

_____

_____

_____

_____

_____

_____

_____

_____

_____

_____

_____

_____

Most who answer that second question will answer it with an unanimous "yes." The first time that question was posed to me, I answered "yes" right away. For a very long time, even after becoming a Christian, I felt as if no one had ever experienced the alienation that I was experiencing. I felt like not only was I at a disadvantage because I desired to leave a homosexual lifestyle, but also I was doubly burdened because no one else had to fight off temptations like I did that tried to drag me back to that lifestyle.

When we feel alone in our struggles and temptations, it is always good to turn to the Word of God. It is a real comfort, especially when it seems as if no one around understands. 1 Corinthians 10:13 reads, "But no temptation has overtaken you except such as is common to man; but God is faithful, who will not allow you to be tempted beyond what you are able, but with the temptation will also make the way of escape, that you may be able to bear it." That is an interesting phrase—"common to man"—but what does it mean? The NLT reads this way: "But remember that the temptations that come into your life are no different from what others experience."

I want you to understand that the temptations that you experience, even the ones that lead you towards sexual immorality, are common to man, experienced by men across the world. You are not alone, and you are not the exception. You are simply a man being battered by an enemy who is out to destroy you and a sin nature that is out to lead you in ways you don't want to go.

Please don't think that any of the things you feel are anything new. Man has been tempted to live outside of God's will in regards to sex and sexuality since the dawn of time. One example in the Bible, although not the first, was King David. He was a man known for pursuing God, but yet and still, he was a man. In the story of his sin with Bathsheba, we see that he was so filled with lust for her that he was willing to kill her husband to get her.

Earlier than this, we have the famous story of the fall of Sodom and Gomorrah. We see here that the men of these cities were so filled with lust that they wanted to have homosexual sex with angels.

In the New Testament, we see Jesus Christ Himself being tempted by Satan, immediately after being baptized. Here we only see three temptations, none of which are recorded as sexual in nature, but they were still enticements to do wrong. (See Luke 4:1–13.) We also read of Paul stating that men had been enticed to sin sexually and were yet able to overcome these temptations (1 Corinthians 6:9–11).

When I learned this, when godly men showed me that I was not experiencing anything new, I was able to accept my place in this life, no longer condemned to something I had no control over.

As we move on, I encourage you to take the time to pray about temptation. Ingest this teaching, because in it you will find the strength to continue to fight.

Personal Space

In light of this teaching on temptation, read Romans 8:1–4. This passage tells us that we are no longer condemned to be subject to the enemy (Satan) or to our sin nature (the flesh) because we are in Christ Jesus. Write out a prayer asking God to make this clear to you, asking Him to make you confident of this very thought—because in the next section, we will learn how and why we fight.

_____

_____

_____

_____

_____

_____

_____

_____

_____

_____

_____

_____

PART 2

For though we walk in the flesh, we do not war according to the flesh. For the weapons of our warfare are not carnal but mighty in God for pulling down strongholds, casting down arguments and every high thing that exalts itself against the knowledge of God, bringing every thought into captivity to the obedience of Christ.

—1 Corinthians 10:3–5

Section Goals:

- To learn how to fight against temptation.
- To be equipped to recognize temptation when it rears its ugly head.
- To recognize that God's grace is sufficient for the battle against homosexuality.
- To memorize 1 Corinthians 10:3–5.

In the last section, we learned about what temptation is and where it comes from. Now, we are going to learn how to fight it.

This is an area that gave me a lot of trouble when I first began this journey. Even though my homosexual activity was in the closet, it was my lifeline to the things that gave me peace, however elusive or short-lived it was. Fighting against temptation became hard for me because the temptations looked so familiar, so comfortable. I could not, and often did not want to, destroy and kill the things I had come to love. But in that lifestyle, the cons outweighed the pros, so I came to accept that if I was ever going to be free from

them, I was going to have to start waging war. This is how
I did it: there were three things I had to learn:

1. How to run *away* from temptation.
2. How to run *towards* God for help.
3. How to *equip* myself to fight temptation off when it
   came too close.

Running Away

In a Bible study I participated in, I learned this concept of
running away. It comes from Genesis 39:1–11 (all emphasis
my own):

> Now Joseph had been taken down to Egypt. And
> Potiphar, an officer of Pharaoh, captain of the guard,
> an Egyptian, bought him from the Ishmaelites who had
> taken him down there.
>
> The Lord was with Joseph, and he was a success-
> ful man; and he was in the house of his master the
> Egyptian.
>
> And his master saw that the Lord was with him and
> that the Lord made all he did to prosper in his hand.
>
> So Joseph found favor in his sight, and served him.
> Then he made him overseer of his house, all that he had
> he put under his authority.
>
> So it was, from the time that he had made him overseer
> of his house and all that he had, that the Lord blessed the
> Egyptian's house for Joseph's sake; and the blessing of
> the Lord was on all that he had in the house and in the
> field.

Thus he left all that he had in Joseph's hand, and he did not know what he had except for the bread which he ate. Now Joseph was handsome in form and appearance.

And it came to pass after these things that his master's wife cast longing eyes on Joseph, and she said, "Lie with me."

But he refused and said to his master's wife, "Look, my master does not know what is with me in the house, and he has committed all that he has to my hand. There is no one greater in this house than I, nor has he kept back anything from me but you, because you are his wife. *How then can I do this great wickedness, and sin against God?*"

So it was, as she spoke to Joseph *day by day*, that he did not heed her, to lie with her or to be with her.

But it happened about this time, when Joseph went into the house to do his work, and none of the men of the house was inside, that she caught him by his garment, saying, "Lie with me." *But he left his garment in her hand, and fled and ran outside.*

There are so many strong points to make about this passage, but let me start with what I think is the strongest: Who was Joseph thinking about when faced with the temptation to sleep with Potiphar's wife?

Go back into the verses and circle the word "God."

Now, if you have a highlighter handy, highlight the word "God."

Joseph was highly blessed by God. These verses tell us that in Egypt, a land where the God of Israel was not honored, Potipher's land was still blessed and allowed to prosper because of the relationship that Joseph had with God. Everything Joseph's hand touched was blessed. I think that Joseph understood that all he had and all he was came from the God he worshipped. So he was very careful about not wanting to sin against God, even when something as beautiful as the wife of his employer wanted to sleep with him.

Joseph kept God on his mind and at the forefront of everything he did so that God would be pleased with him. This led to his being equipped to flee from temptation. Just like it was for Joseph, it is extremely important for you to understand that keeping your mind stayed on God will keep you in times of temptation.

Before we move forward with these verses in Genesis, let's look at what happens when God is not kept at the forefront.

Psalm 51 is one of the prayers of David, King of Israel. Verses three and four read,

"For I acknowledge my transgressions, and my sin is always before me. *Against You, You only, have I sinned,* and done this evil in your sight—that you may be found just when you speak and blameless when you judge" (emphasis my own).

The story behind this prayer is found 2 Samuel 11. It is the story of how David was so overcome with lust for Bathsheba, another man's wife, that he first lusted after her, slept with her, got her pregnant and then was willing to abuse his power as king and have her husband killed so that he could marry her. It is the story of sexual temptation beating a man down low enough to sin against God. Luckily, David saw and finally acknowledged the error of his ways and repented.

In verse four of Psalm 51, who does David say that he sinned against?

_____

That's right: GOD. David saw that even though he had killed a man and taken his wife, his ultimate sin was against God.

Read 2 Samuel 11:2–4. Do these verses mention that David focused on God at any time during his temptation? No, they don't. But we do see that David was overtaken by Bathsheba's beauty and immediately went out about scheming to get her into bed. And we also see in Psalm 51, when he began to repent, David realized that, ultimately, the Person he had hurt the most was God.

Both sides of this issue have happened to me plenty of times. In the times I remained strong in the face of sleeping with some man or entering some porn store, I know that it was because I immediately began to think about how much it would hurt God and how much damage I would do after all the time I had spent on the journey. And in the times when I fell into sin, it was because I took my eyes off God and was more interested in getting off than staying pure.

Personal Space

Has this ever happened to you? If you have been on the journey for a while, do you think your victories came about because you kept your eyes on God? If you haven't, do you think your slip-ups were because you had nothing righteous or godly to keep your eyes on? Write down some thoughts related to these questions.

_____

_____

_____

_____

_____

_____

_____

_____

_____

_____

_____

_____

_____

_____

_____

Jude 24 says, "Now to Him who is able to keep you from stumbling and to present youfaultless before the presence of His glory with exceeding joy…" In this verse, the author, Jude, is giving praise to our Savior for His ability to keep us from falling or stumbling. Do you think Jude could write such beautiful words if his focus wasn't on God? I don't. In order for God to be able to do this for us (and I believe with my entire being that this is His desire), we have to keep focused on Him and keep abiding in Him so that when temptation comes, our eyes won't be on what our senses might want but on the One who can keep us pure and standing upright.

This brings us back to Joseph. The second point I wanted to make about this passage is that we see temptation badgering him, gnawing at him like a dog at a bone.

Look at verse ten of the passage from Genesis. How frequently was Potiphar's wife harassing Joseph to sleep with her?

_____

For most of us, it is not hard to imagine Joseph being tempted from left, right, top, and bottom day after endless day, because that's the way it works for us, too.

In the city I used to live in, I encountered my very first porn store that had "interactive" viewing booths. And guess where that store was located? Right on my commute to work. Every day, I had to either ride or walk by that store. And every day, I saw men going in and out, most wearing stressed-out frowns on the way in and relaxed smiles on the way out. Do you know how hard it was for me to resist that place on a daily basis? *Very hard.* Some days I would make it past by the skin of my teeth and on other days—let's just say I didn't make it past.

Temptation is very persistent. In the New Testament, we read that even Jesus was tempted. He was tempted by the devil himself and overcame the temptation. The Scriptures say that the devil backed off until there was more opportune time to resume the temptation (Luke 4:13). Now if Jesus was constantly tempted, what makes you think you won't be?

Finally, we come to the last thing that is so powerful about our story with Joseph.

Look at the passage in Genesis 39 again. What jumps out at you from the last sentence in Genesis 39:12?

_____

_____

_____

Joseph *ran* from the temptation. And not only did he run, but also he ran in such haste that he left his garment behind!

In our society, to run away from a situation is portrayed as being weak. But I would beg to differ and would say to you that when you are faced with temptation, homosexual or otherwise, running does not show cowardice. It shows determination to do the will of God—determination not to sin. And if you happen to leave something behind as you make your exit, leave it.

To reiterate this, read 1 Corinthians 6:18. What does it tell you to do?

_____

Flee. Run. Jet. Scram. HIGH TAIL IT OUT OF THERE!

Too many of us want to be able to look temptation in the face and stand our ground. But that is not the way God intended you to fight. He wants you to look to Him and run in the opposite direction of the temptation. White-knuckling it through will only weaken you and make you more susceptible to giving in.

> If you run in the opposite direction of the temptation, you will be running TOWARDS the exact opposite of the temptation: God Himself.

Running Towards God

Let's look at Hebrews 2:18. The NIV reads, "Because he himself [Jesus] suffered when he was tempted, he is able to aid those who are being tempted."

What two things happened to Christ in this verse?
He _____ and He was _____.

Suffering and temptation go hand in hand. What does it say that He is able to do because of this?
He is able to _____who are being tempted.

In the churches that I have been a part of, it has always been said that those best qualified to minister to a specific need are those who have had that need in the past. In Alcoholics Anonymous, recovered alcoholics are the ones who lead and facilitate groups. In our study here, I, a man who is journeying on the road out of homosexuality, seek to minister to you, someone who may be starting or seeking to maintain a journey on that road.

In Hebrews 2:18, we see that Christ is qualified to aid all of us in our times of temptation because He Himself suffered and was tempted. Shouldn't this encourage us to run after Him? He knows what we are going through and felt the feelings we feel, isn't that enough to run to Him for help?

Let's look at Hebrews 14:16, another verse that reiterates this: "Seeing then that we have a great High Priest who has passed through the heavens, Jesus the Son of God, let us hold fast our confession. *For we do not have a High Priest who cannot sympathize with our weaknesses, but was in all points tempted as we are,* yet without sin. *Let us therefore come boldly to the throne of grace, that we may obtain mercy and find grace to help in time of need"* (emphasis my own).

Highlight the phrase, "but was in all points tempted as we are." Again, we see that Christ knows what it is like to be tempted. He was tempted for forty days in the wilderness by the devil and even after that, tempted whenever the devil could find an "opportune time"(Luke 4:1–13).

Now here is the exciting part about this verse. It says "therefore," meaning that because of everything just said (namely Christ being our High Priest who is able to sympathize with our weaknesses), we can come *boldly* before the throne of grace in order to find and obtain help. *Boldly*—that is a strong word. To me, it implies that we have a *right*. That because of all of this, we have permission to come and are entitled to help. This gives us all the more reason to run to Him in times of trouble.

Personal Space

Record your reactions to the following verses in light of our discussion on running towards God:

The name of the Lord is a strong tower; the righteous run to and are safe. (Proverbs 18:10)

_____

_____

_____

_____

Come to Me, all you who labor and are heavy laden, and I will give you rest. Take My yoke upon you and learn from Me, for I am gentle and lowly in heart, and your will find rest for your souls. For My yoke is easy and My burden is light. (Matthew 11:28–30)

_____

_____

_____

_____

Therefore He is also able to save to the uttermost those who come to God through Him, since He always lives to make intercession for them. (Hebrews 7:25)

_____

_____

_____

_____

Equipping Yourself

In any fight, we know that in order to be effective, one has to be equipped. You have to have the right tools for the right job. Spiritual warfare against temptation is no different. I am so glad that God has not left us unfitted for war. He has given us the tools necessary for battle.

Earlier in the first section on temptation, we looked at the two natures of temptation: our enemy, the devil, and our own sin nature. Now we are going to examine the tools needed to fight both of them off.

Let's start with the devil. In Temptation Part 1, we looked at Ephesians 6:12. Let's expand our look at it to include more of the chapter. Look at Ephesians 6:10–18:

Finally , be strong in the Lord, and in the strength of His might. Put on the full armor of God, that you may be able to stand firm against the schemes of the devil. For our struggle is not against flesh and blood, but against the rulers, against the powers, against the world forces of this darkness, against the spiritual forces of wickedness in the heavenly places. Therefore take up the full armor of God, so that you may be able to resist in the evil day, and having done everything, to stand firm. Stand firm therefore, having girded your loins with truth, and having put on the breastplate of righteousness, and having shod your feet with the preparation of the Gospel of Peace; in addition to all, taking up the shield of faith with which you will be able to extinguish all the flaming missiles of the evil one. And take the helmet of salvation, and the sword of the Spirit, which is the word of God. With all prayer and petition pray at all times in the Spirit, and with this in view, be on the alert with all perseverance and petition for all the saints.

—NASB

Whew. That's a mouthful. But it is so packed with power! The full armor of God is such a powerful set of equipment. The apostle Paul's words here do these three things:

1. They *encourage*: The very first verse tells us to "be strong in the Lord, and in the strength of His might." We are about to venture into battle tactics, and I believe that this particular verse is an encouragement for the battle coming up next.
2. They *expose our enemy*: We have already looked at the fact that the enemy throwing temptations our way is the devil himself. But it is always good to be reminded of it again. Never think for a second that we are fighting against an enemy who is naïve or simple-minded. The devil is a trickster by heart and out to gain our destruction. Don't underestimate him. You have to be ready for his tactics at all times.

3. They *equip us for battle*: Here is the meat of the verses! Here is where we find the things that are going to protect us.

We are going to look at these items for battle one by one. But before we do, we need to recognize something. Each part of the armor is either a weapon or a tool of protection. So, we see that they do one of two things: they either protect a body part (defensive tactics) or they are used aggressively in combat (offensive tactics).

Now, as we go through the list, fill in the blanks and match up either the tool of protection with the body part it protects or the weapon with the fight tactic.

1. Having girded your _____ with _____
   (verse 14). Truth is the first tool of protection that we are given, and the verse tells us to "stand firm, having girded our loins" with it. The NLT paraphrases it: "putting on the sturdy belt of truth." The NIV translates it: "with the belt of truth buckled around your waist." The truth of God's Word is to be tied to us, tethered to our bodies so that it goes everywhere with us.

2. Having put on the _____ of _____
   (verse 14). There is a paraphrased version of the Bible called *Word on the Street*[1] by Rob Lacey that I think explains this part of the verse very well. It reads, "with your bulletproof vest of right lifestyle fixed on tight." That is awesome. We have to be attempting to live as righteously as possible in order to ask God

for something. Yes, we make mistakes—but we can't be making them on purpose and still expect God to bless us. Strap the breastplate around your chest, and you won't ever have to fight without it.

3. Having _____ your _____ with the preparation of the _____ of _____ (verse 15). The NLT reads, "For shoes, put on the peace that comes from the Good News." A modern way to say this might be, "Everywhere you go, tell someone about what Jesus has done in your life." We will talk later about using our overcoming testimony as a witness for God, but here you need to understand that when you speak about the goodness of God and the awesomeness of the gospel (or Good News), you are waging war against the enemy. He hates to hear the news of forgiveness of sins being found in Christ Jesus. And talking about this will keep you from wanting to sin sexually or otherwise.

4. In addition to all, taking up the _____ of _____ with which you will be able to _____ all the _____ of the evil one (verse 16). Your belief in Christ Jesus is going to take you far. If you hold onto it, believe it, and cherish it, even when it is hard to do so, that faith will kill the giants in your life. You will be able to say no to that random hook up because your faith is telling you that "greater is He that is in you than he that is in the world" (1 John 4:4). The shield of faith will protect you from the things that people say and

do that do not line up with the Word of God. When someone says, "Well, we will always sin, so there is no point in trying not to," your faith in Christ and His Word will tell you, "Nay, in all these things, we are more than conquerors through Him that loved us" (Romans 8:37 KJV). Believe and keep the faith. It will keep you in times of trouble.

5. And take the _____ of _____ and the _____ of the _____ which is the _____ of _____ (verse 17). There are two things that should mean more than the world to you: your salvation and the Word of God. Both of these are more valuable than any treasure on earth. Your salvation is the very basis on which the rest stands—if Christ did not rise from the dead and if He did not save you from your sins, you are still lost. Fortunately, we know that He did both of those things. And the Word of God is our road map to eternal life. Psalm 119:9 says, "How can a young man cleanse his way? By taking heed according to Your word," and Psalm 119:105 says, "Your word is a lamp to my feet and a light to my path." The Word of God is going to be around and stand true way past the end of the world; you can count on it remaining true, pure, and relevant. Hebrews 4:12 says, "the word of God is living and powerful, and sharper than any two-edged sword, piercing even to the division of soul and spirit, and of joints and marrow, and is a discerner of the thoughts and intents of the heart." It is powerful. Second Timothy 3:16–17 says, "All

Scripture is given by inspiration of God, and is profitable for doctrine, for reproof, for correction, for instruction in righteousness, that the man of God may be complete, *thoroughly equipped* for every good work" (emphasis my own). The Word of God can teach you and equip you to fight and to remain righteous.

6. With all _____, pray at all times in the _____ (verse 18). Staying in communication with God is key if you are going to know what weapon to whip out or which defense to throw up. In times when you are faced with the opportunity to sin that seems so appealing but you know is so wrong in the eyes of God, you are going to need to pray in order to see the avenue of escape. This verse tells you to connect to God in prayer and petition through the Spirit of God Himself at *all times*. There will never come a day when you don't need to seek God for guidance. First Thessalonians 5:17 tells you simply to "pray without ceasing."

7. And with this in view, be on the _____ with all perseverance and _____ for all the _____ (verse 18). Be ready at all times to pray for your brothers (and sisters) in the body of Christ. This verse is showing us that petitions or prayers are always needed for the Church across the world, because we all need each other. If we all pray for each other all the time, we know that at all times, someone somewhere is praying on our behalf. I am always praying for you. Please do the same for me.

James 5:16 says to "confess your trespasses to one another and pray for one another, that you may be healed. The effective, fervent prayer of a righteous man avails much" (emphasis my own).

Personal Space

Take the time to write out precise steps you can take to implement each piece of the armor of God into your life. How can you pray more? How can you increase your faith? How can you talk more about the gospel? Is there an area of truth in the Bible that you struggle with? Go through each of the pieces and figure out how you can increase in using/ implemented each one.

_____

_____

_____

_____

_____

_____

_____

_____

_____

_____

_____

_____

_____

_____

_____

_____

There is one final aspect to being equipped against temptation that I want to make you aware of. I want you to understand that there are some things in life that we deal with and fight against because God has *allowed* them to be there. He does not create temptation, nor does He tempt us with it (James 1:13–14), but He does allow for some things to be present so that we can recognize that we have to depend on God for victory over our battles.

Let's look at 2 Corinthians 12:7–9:

> So to keep me from becoming proud, I was given a thorn in my flesh, a messenger from Satan to torment me and keep me from becoming proud. Three different times I begged the Lord to take it away. Each time He said, "My grace is all you need. My power works best in weakness." So now I am glad to boast about my weaknesses, so that the power of Christ can work through me.

Paul is telling us in this passage that God had allowed an intense temptation (a messenger of Satan) to work in his life so that he would not become proud. He asked God to take it away from him on numerous occasions.

What is God's answer to Paul?

TEMPTATION • 87

———————————
———————————
———————————
———————————

God tells Paul that His grace is all he needs, that His power works best in weakness. The New King James Version puts it this way: "My grace is sufficient."

Did you get that? God is telling Paul, and telling you, that His grace is enough to keep you from falling. If He simply took your struggle away, you might not look to God and be dependent on Him. God tells you, as the reader of this verse, that when you are at your weakest, when you recognize that the lifestyle of homosexuality is not something that you can control and that you can change on your own, then you will be forced to look to Him for help. God wants you to depend on Him.

My friend, I have told you before that I do believe in a God who is powerful enough to do a supernatural feat in your life. If He chooses to, He can wipe every taste for homosexual sex from your appetite. But I need you to be ready for the possibility of that not happening. I need you to understand that your taste for homosexuality may be the thing that God wants to use to make sure that you look to Him for all your help and guidance. Does that seem a little arrogant on God's part? Maybe a little. But remember this: He gave you the life that you live. He gave you the air you breathe and the clothes you wear, and He can give you the sexuality you desire.

If it doesn't happen that all homosexual temptations are zapped out of your life, you must understand that that does not mean that you are not free. You can choose God in the face of temptation. Remember that even if the temptation was placed there to keep you dependent on God, He still always provides the "way of escape" (1 Corinthians 10:13).

I do not know if homosexuality is your "thorn in the flesh." For me, it is. I still am tempted when I see an attractive man, but I can now walk in the freedom of choosing how I respond. For you, it may be a thorn that will disappear, or it may not. But just know that there is that way of escape and that the thorn is present in order that the "power of Christ may work in you."

Now, as we end this section on temptation, I want you to take another look at the opening memory verse, 1 Corinthians 10:3–5: "For though we walk in the flesh, we do not war according to the flesh. For the weapons of our warfare are not carnal but mighty in God for pulling down strongholds, casting down arguments and every high thing that exalts itself against the knowledge of God, bringing every thought into captivity to the obedience of Christ…"

We have learned battle strategies for fighting temptation. But I want us to keep in mind the goal that we should have when we fight. There is the immediate goal of simply getting out of the temptation and overcoming it, but what about the future? Do we simply want to get over it and leave it festering, possibly to rear its ugly head again? No, I don't think we do. I say this because that is how I functioned for the first of couple years of the journey. I was so tired of excessive fornication, masturbation, and porn usage that I simply wanted to get past the temptation, not kill it. But our memory verse takes us beyond the immediate. It shows us that our fighting not only allows us to jump over or go around the temptation, but also to kill it, to destroy it, to cast it down.

These temptations we face are more than just issues to get over. They are strongholds, shackles. They are arguments that try to debate their validity with God. We need to cast them down. Why? Because when we cast them down, we see a greater result. We see that we are *bringing every thought into captivity to the obedience of Christ.* We are making our temptations obey the Word of our Lord and Savior. When we cast them down, when we take the time to make sure that we are equipped and always on the battlefield, we are making them stay in place. While we will always face temptations, I believe that they shouldn't always be as strong as they were yesterday. If I overcome an invitation to sleep around today and I pass the test, giving God glory and remaining rooted in Him, tomorrow that temptation should have less of a hold on me. I should be able to say, "Nope, I can't go there. I may fall into something else, but God brought me out of this yesterday, He can do the same today."

I am not saying we will never fall again but simply that if we slay the beast, take extra measures to make sure he is good and dead, it is more likely that he won't rear his head the same way tomorrow. For me, those extra measures included changing my commute to work when I had to ride past that porn store everyday, so that tomorrow, I wouldn't be tempted like I was today.

Personal Space

Take the time to evaluate your motives. Do you just want to get past the temptation, or do you want to slay the beast? You may find that you're not ready for the slaying yet, and if you aren't, write out a prayer to God asking for that power. If you are ready and willing, thank God for allowing you to be so.

_____

_____

_____

_____

_____

_____

_____

_____

_____

_____

_____

_____

I pray every temptation in your life will be destroyed as you learn to fight with the full armor of God.

CHAPTER 8

RECONCILIATION: TRAVELING BACK HOME

Likewise I say to you, there is joy in the presence of the angels of God over one sinner who repents.

—Luke 15:10

"For this my son was dead and is alive again; he was lost and is found." And they began to be merry.

—Luke 15:24

Section Goals:

- To understand that reconciliation with God and the body of Christ is always possible, even after falling into sin.
- To understand the fullness of the grace of God—that it is not just something that brings salvation but that it can forgive our pitfalls and mistakes as believers.
- To memorize Luke 15:10, 24.

I WANT TO SHARE with you a devotional I was fortunate enough to have published on the web by The Christian Broadcast Network, better known as CBN.

There was a time when I thought that my marriage would not last forever. After years of investment, my wife and I considered separation because of an addiction I had to sexual sin. And not only was I locked into a bondage that caused me to commit adultery but it was also with members of my own gender.

The life of sin was so binding that after a lot of self-evaluation, I came to the conclusion that as my spouse, she did not deserve the pain and humiliation that I was causing her. So, after not being able to suppress my conscience, I told her about the current act I had committed and that because I loved her and wanted to see her happy, I wanted her to move on and build a life for herself, where she did not have to be subject to this kind of hurt. I was going to leave until I could get my life under control and if God was merciful, she would be willing and free to reconcile.

It was at this point that I learned that grace is more than unmerited favor. It is a demonstration of God's love even when we, His children, act extremely unlovable.

In the book of Romans Paul wrote these words:

For when we were still without strength, in due time Christ died for the ungodly . . . .But God demonstrates His own love toward us, in that while we were still sinners, Christ died for us.

—Romans 5:6, 8

With my wife's next words, she demonstrated to me the depth and reality of God's love. She told me that even though she was in pain, even though logic was telling her to leave me for good, she loved me enough to bear the pain, maintain our marriage, and see me come to the freedom that God would grant to me if I continued to seek Him. She told me that she loved God, she loved me, and that that love would keep her here as long as I was willing to try.

I was floored. Never before, even in my Christian walk, had I known such a selfless love. She was willing to endure the pain of knowing that her husband had an addiction that he could not control and that until God was able to penetrate his heart, his will, and his sin, there was the chance that she might be hurt again.

And she still wanted to stay. For God, for me, and for our marriage.

This is the nature of God. Even though we are ungodly, depraved sinners at best, He loves us enough to put up with us in the condition we are in. He knows that "all our righteousnesses are like filthy rags" (Isaiah 64:6), and without His Son's blood paying the price for our sins we are lost.

Everyone on earth has sinned. Not only does the Bible say so, but every one of us knows that if we would honestly evaluate ourselves, each one of us has been disobedient to God. No matter how hard we may try to be and do good, we can't because our sin nature is in opposition to God's plan for our lives. Whether or not it is sexual sin, we all have something that if left unchecked will build a wall up between God and us, thus breaking fellowship and hindering our relationship.

We must accept the fact that without the God of the universe taking complete control of our lives and hopefully granting us pardon for our wayward ways, we will fail at being righteous in our own power, every time.

Fortunately, His Son's blood and His Son's pain cover our sins and make the way for Grace to abound. Today, I am still married and free from sin and addiction, because of God's Grace.

During the time described above, I did not understand the concept of reconciliation—not with my wife and certainly not with God. I was so bound by depression and negative thinking because of committing adultery that I could not fathom the possibility of either my wife or of my God wanting anything to do with me ever again.

I want you to know that this is a lie from the pit of hell. Satan does not want us to know and accept the fact that when we fall, God's arms are always stretched wide open to receive us if we run back to Him.

We see this best played out in the famous story of the Prodigal Son told in Luke 15:11–24. This is the story of a wayward child, a child so fixed on material possessions and lusts that he chose to spend the inheritance that was to be granted to him by his father on frivolous stuff. I can imagine him indulging in cruises and vacations, buying jewelry and expensive clothes. If I were him, I would have probably been spending it on pay-per-view porn sites and homosexual activities.

Verse 14 tells us that when he had done something, he began to be in real need. What was it that he did?

_____

_____

The New King James Version says that he "spent all." He took all that his father had given him and spent it on all of these extravagant, maybe even lustful and homosexual, tastes.

Personal Space

Have you "spent all"? Have you spent all of your time, talent, energy, and resources trying to make homosexuality work? If so, are you ready to give it up? Write down some thoughts about your desire and readiness to turn away from the homosexual lifestyle and its temptations.

_____

_____

_____

_____

_____

_____

_____

_____

_____

Eventually, the prodigal son was ready to give up and go back home. He had found as he lived frivolously that no one was around to help him in his time of need. He ended up having to lease himself to a local man in the country he had moved to in order to find a job just to survive.

But thank God he had a revelation!

Read verses 17 and 18. What does it say that he realized?

_____

_____

_____

_____

He realized that he had sinned. He saw his sin of disobedient living as what it was at its core—a sin against God. What he realized is an illustration of what a truly repentant man should feel in his heart. (Read through Psalm 51 again.)

What did the son decide to do?

_____

_____

He decided to go back to his father. He decided that he would bond himself to his father, no longer as a son but as a servant. He saw that because of his sin, he wasn't worthy of sonship.

Now here is the beautiful thing about this story. The father rejoiced over his son's return and *restored him to his previous position.*

You are the prodigal son. I am the prodigal son. We need constantly to remind ourselves of this and remember that if we return to God when we make a mistake, He will *restore us.* He will reconcile with us.

I stated before that you are bound to sin. It's just a part of life. But God wants you to come home! If while on the road to freedom you slip and view some porn or sleep around, don't let that keep you away from God! He desires that you repent and that you realize that He wants you home and in your proper place.

When I fell into adultery, I almost gave up on my marriage, because I didn't think that reconciliation was possible. I gave up on God because I didn't think He wanted anything to do with someone who couldn't stand up to temptation. I didn't think that my wife wanted anything to do with me, either. But I was wrong on both accounts. Through my wife's act of selflessness and love, I saw that the grace of God makes a way for reconciliation, even when it looks impossible.

You can always come back home. When you sin, don't let it stop you. Let it motivate you never to fall into that same temptation again. And because you can always come back home, this means that you always have a place in the church as well. While I know that some may have been hurt by well-meaning Christians who don't understand that we are called to reconcile prodigals back to the body of Christ, I don't believe that all churches are like that. At least mine isn't. We take seriously Galatians 6:1–2, which says, "Brethren, if a man is overtaken in a trespass, you who are spiritual restore such a one in a spirit of gentleness, considering yourself lest you also be tempted. Bear one another's burdens, and so fulfill the law of Christ."

I still believe that there are churches across the world that are waiting to welcome you with open arms back into the body of believers if you happen to stray away or fall into sin. If one church hurts you, try the next. And if that one hurts you, come to mine. The church is called—better yet, *required*—to love you. You always have a place in the body.

Second Corinthians 5:20 says, "Now then, we are ambassadors for Christ, as though God were pleading through us: we implore you on Christ's behalf, *be reconciled to God*" (Emphasis my own). Hebrews 4:16 tells us this: "Let us therefore come boldly to the throne of grace, that we may obtain mercy and find grace to help in time of need." God is there to grant forgiveness and mercy if you just run to Him in your time of need. Believe this: temptation will kill you if you don't let God either keep you from it or forgive you for giving into it.

Personal Space

Where are you with this? If you are a prodigal right now, will you please come back home? Take this space to

pray to our Father and ask Him for either reconciliation or
the strength and power to remember that reconciliation is
always possible, even if you stray.

_____

_____

_____

_____

_____

_____

_____

_____

_____

_____

_____

_____

_____

_____

_____

I pray that you will always see God as the Father who
wants you to come home. God and His angels have a praise
party every time one of us comes back. Praise the Lord!

CHAPTER 9

IDENTIFY YOURSELF: KNOWING WHO YOU ARE IN CHRIST

Therefore, if anyone is in Christ, he is a new creation; old things have passed away; behold, all things become new.

—Corinthians 5:17

Chapter Goals:

- To begin to understand what your new identity is in Christ.
- To memorize 2 Corinthians 5:17.

IT MAY NOT look like it sometimes, but God gave you a new identity when you came to Christ. You are no longer what you used to be, and you are becoming something totally new. Despite what anyone says, you don't have to identify yourself with homosexuality if you are on the road towards freedom. God has made you a new creation.

In this section, I have no desire to pass out personal advice. When I began to see and believe my new identity in Christ, it wasn't through a counselor or a mentor or some author. It was through the Word of God. I immersed myself in what the Word of God had to say about who I am and who I am not. Because society is sometimes going to condemn you and not believe your testimony of being able to come out of a homosexual lifestyle, you need to be so grounded in the Word of God that nothing will be able to dissuade you from believing it.

So here's what we're going to do. Let's spend some serious time examining our identities in Christ, not as a product of my own opinion but as a product of time spent in the Word. This section is made up entirely of Personal Space just for that purpose.

Personal space

In the following blank spaces, insert your name in order to complete the affirmation of identity given. Then read the verses that follow. After every 20 verses, there will be space for you to react to any verses that stood out to you.

_____ is able—Philippians 4:13

_____ is abounding in grace—2 Corinthians 9:8

_____ is abounding in hope—Romans 15:4, 13

_____ is accepted—Ephesians 1:6

_____ has access—Ephesians 2:18

_____ is adequate—2 Corinthians 3:5

_____ is adopted—Ephesians 1:5

_____ is alive—Ephesians 2:4–5

_____ is an ambassador for Christ—2 Corinthians 5:20

_____ is anointed—1 John 2:20

_____ is the apple of His eye—Zechariah 2:8

_____ is appointed by God—John 15:16

_____ is not ashamed—2 Timothy 1:12

_____ is assured of reward—1 Corinthians 15:58

_____ is assured of success—Proverbs 16:3

_____ has authority over the devil—Luke 9:1

_____ is baptized into Christ—Corinthians 12:15

_____ is becoming a mature person—Ephesians 4:13

_____ is becoming conformed to Christ—Romans 8:29

_____ is a believer—Romans 10:9

_____ belongs to God—John 17:9

_____ is blameless—1 Corinthians 1:8

_____ is blessed—Ephesians 1:3

_____ is blood bought—1 Corinthians 6:19–20

_____ is bold—Proverbs 28:1

_____ is a bondservant—Psalm 116:16

_____ is born of God—1 John 5:18

_____ is born again—1 Peter 1:23

_____ is bought with a price—1 Corinthians 6:20

_____ is a branch of the True Vine—John 15:5

_____ is His bride—Isaiah 54:5

_____ is His brother—Hebrews 2:11

_____ is brought near—Ephesians 2:13

_____ is built up—1 Peter 2:5

_____ is buried with Christ—Romans 6:4

_____ is called—1 Peter 5:10

_____ is cared for—1 Peter 5:7

_____ is carried—Exodus 19:4

_____ is changed—1 Samuel 10:6

_____ is a child of God—John 1:12

Which verse sticks out the most to you and why?

_____

_____

_____

_____

_____

_____ is cherished—Ephesians 5:29

_____ is chosen—1 Peter 2:9

_____ is a citizen of heaven—Philippians 3:20

_____ is clay in the potter's hand—Jeremiah 18:6

_____ is clean—Ezekiel 36:25; John 15:3

_____ is cleansed—1 John 1:7, 9

_____ is clothed with Christ—Galatians 3:27

_____ is a co-heir with Christ—Romans 8:17

_____ is comforted—Jeremiah 31:13

_____ is complete in Christ—Colossians 2:10

_____ is confident—1 John 4:17

_____ is confident of answers to prayer—1 John 5:14–15

_____ is confident He will finish His good work in me—Philippians 1:6

_____ is confident He will never leave me—Hebrews 13:5–6

_____ is a conqueror—Romans 8:37

_____ is content with weakness—2 Corinthians 12:10

_____ is continually with God—Psalm 73:23

_____ is controlled by the love of Christ—2 Corinthians 12:10

_____ is created in Christ for good works—Ephesians 2:10

_____ is created in His image—Genesis 1:27

_____ is crucified with Him—Galatians 2:20

_____ is dead to sin—Romans 6:11

_____ is delighted in—Isaiah 42:1

_____ is delivered—Psalm 107:6

_____ is desired—Psalm 45:11

_____ is determined and able—Philippians 4:13

_____ is a disciple—John 8:31–32

_____ is disciplined—Hebrews 12:5–11

_____ is drawing near with confidence—Hebrews 4:16

_____ is empowered to obey—Philippians 2:13

_____ is encouraged—2 Thessalonians 2:16–17

_____ is enlightened—Ephesians 1:18

_____ is enriched in everything—1 Corinthians 1:5

_____ is equipped—2 Timothy 3:16–17

_____ is established—Deuteronomy 28:9

_____ has eternal life—John 3:36

_____ has every good thing—Philemon 6

_____ is faithful—Revelation 17:14

_____ is in God's family—Psalm 68:5

Write out a prayer to God asking Him for help with identifying yourself with the truths in the previous verses.

_____

_____

_____

_____

_____

_____ is far from oppression—Isaiah 54:14

_____ is favored—Job 10:12

_____ is a fellow citizen with the saints—Ephesians 2:19

_____ is filled—Acts 2:4

_____ is filled to the fullness of God—Colossians
2:9–10

_____ is filled with the fruit of righteousness—
Philippians 1:11

_____ is filled with the fruit of the Spirit—Galatians
5:22–23

_____ is filled with the knowledge of His will—
Colossians 1:9

_____ is filled with joy—John 17:13

_____ is a finished product-in progress—Philippians
1:6

_____ is a first fruit—Romans 8:23

_____ is forgiven—Ephesians 1:7

_____ was formed in the womb by God—Jeremiah
1:5

_____ was lost, but now is found—Luke 19:10

_____ is free—John 8:36

_____ is freely given all things—Romans 8:32

_____ is gifted—Romans 12:6

_____ is given His magnificent promises—2 Peter
1:3–4

_____ is given His Holy Spirit—2 Corinthians 1:22

_____ is glorified with Him—2 Thessalonians 2:14

_____ is God's child—John 1:12

_____ is God's gift to Christ—John 17:24

_____ knows God is for me—Romans 8:31

_____ is granted grace in Christ Jesus—Romans 5:17, 20

_____ is guarded by God—2 Timothy 1:12

_____ is guarded by God's peace—Philippians 4:7

_____ is guaranteed—Ephesians 1:13–14

_____ is guided—Psalm 48:14

_____ is guiltless—Romans 8:1

_____ is healed—1 Peter 2:24

_____ is healthy—Deuteronomy 7:15

_____ is an heir of God—Titus 3:7

_____ is helped by Him—Isaiah 44:2

_____ is hidden with Christ in God—Colossians 3:3

_____ is His—Isaiah 43:1

_____ is His handiwork—Ephesians 2:10

_____ is holy—Ephesians 1:4

_____ is honored—2 Timothy 2:21

_____ is humble—Philippians 2:24

Write down your thoughts and reactions.

_____

_____

_____

_____

_____ is made in the image of God—Genesis 1:27

_____ is the image and glory of God—1 Corinthians 11:7

_____ is an imitator of God—Ephesians 5:1

_____ is in Christ Jesus—1 Corinthians 1:30

_____ is included—Ephesians 1:13

_____ is indestructible—John 6:51

_____ is indwelt by Christ Jesus—John 14:20

_____ is indwelt by His Spirit—Romans 8:11

_____ is inseparable from His love—Romans 8:35

_____ is an instrument of righteousness—Romans 6:13

_____ is joyful—Philippians 4:4

_____ is justified—Acts 13:39

_____ is kept—Isaiah 38:17

_____ is a king's kid—Psalm 44:4

_____ knows all things work together for good—Romans 8:28

_____ knows in Whom he believes—2 Timothy 1:12

_____ is known—2 Timothy 2:19

_____ lacks no wisdom—James 1:5

_____ is lavished with riches of His grace—Ephesians 1:7–8

_____ is liberated—Romans 6:23

_____ has life abundant—1 John 4:9; John 10:10

_____ has life and peace in the Spirit—Romans 8:6

_____ is a light in a dark place—Acts 13:47

_____ has life flowing through him—John 7:38

_____ is the Lord's—Isaiah 44:5

_____ is loved—John 3:16

_____ is loved constantly, unconditionally—Isaiah 43:4

_____ is loyal—Psalm 86:2

_____ is made by Him—Psalm 100:3

_____ is a magnifier of God—Psalm 69:30

_____ is marked—Ephesians 1:13

_____ is a member of His body—Ephesians 5:30

_____ is mighty in God—Luke 10:19

_____ has the mind of Christ—1 Corinthians 2:16

_____ is a minister—2 Corinthians 3:6

_____ is a minister of reconciliation—2 Corinthians 5:18–19

_____ is a mountain mover—Mark 11:22–23

_____ is near to God—Ephesians 2:13

_____ is never forsaken—Hebrews 13:5

_____ is new—Ephesians 4:24

What are your thoughts and reactions?

_____

_____

_____

_____

_____ is new born—1 Peter 2:2

_____ is a new creation—2 Corinthians 5:17

_____ has new life—Romans 6:4

_____ is not condemned—Romans 8:1

_____ is no longer a slave to sin—Romans 6:6

_____ has not been given a spirit of fear—1 Timothy 1:7

_____ is obedient—Isaiah 1:19

_____ is an object of mercy—Romans 9:23

_____ has obtained an inheritance—Ephesians 1:11

_____ is of God's household—Ephesians 2:19

_____ is on the winning side—Colossians 2:15

_____ is one with Him—John 17:23-24

_____ is an overcomer—1 John 5:4-5

_____ is pardoned—Jeremiah 33:8

_____ is a partaker of Christ—Hebrews 3:14

_____ is a partaker of the Holy Spirit—Hebrews 6:4

_____ is a partaker of grace—Philippians 1:7

_____ is a partaker of the promise in Christ—Ephesians 3:6

_____ has passed from death to life—John 5:24

_____ is patient—James 5:8

_____ has peace—Philippians 4:7

_____ is one of the people of God—1 Peter 2:9

_____ is being perfected—1 Peter 5:10

_____ is pleasing to God—Psalm 149:4

_____ is God's own possession—Titus 2:14

_____ is possessor of all things—1 Corinthians 3:21–23

_____ has the power of God behind him—Philippians 3:21

_____ has power—Acts 1:8

_____ has power over the devil—Luke 9:1

_____ is predestined—Ephesians 1:11

_____ is prepared beforehand for glory—Romans 9:23

_____ is prosperous—Psalm 1:3

_____ is protected—Psalm 91:14

_____ is provided for—Matthew 6:33

_____ is purchased—Revelation 5:9

_____ is purposeful—Psalm 138:8

_____ is qualified—Colossians 1:12

_____ is raised up with Christ—Ephesians 2:6

_____ is ransomed with Him—Isaiah 35:10

_____ is rare—Proverbs 20:15

Pick one of the previous verses and write out what God is telling you in it.

_____

_____

_____

_____

_____

_____ has received mercy—1 Peter 2:10

_____ has received an unshakable kingdom—Hebrews
12:28

_____ is reconciled to God—Romans 5:10

_____ is redeemed—Galatians 3:13

_____ is refined—Isaiah 48:10

_____ is reigning with Him—Romans 5:17

_____ is rejoicing—Romans 5:2–3

_____ is renewed—2 Corinthians 4:16

_____ is His representative—Matthew 5:16

_____ is rescued—Colossians 1:13

_____ has rest provided—Matthew 11:28–30

_____ is rewarded by God—Isaiah 49:4

_____ is rich—2 Corinthians 8:9

_____ is righteous—Ephesians 4:22

_____ is rooted and built up in Him—Colossians 2:7

_____ is royalty—Romans 5:17, 8:16–17

_____ is in a royal priesthood—1 Peter 2:9

_____ is safe—Psalm 4:8

_____ is a saint of God—Psalm 34:9

_____ is the salt of the earth—Matthew 5:13

_____ is sanctified—1 Corinthians 6:11

_____ is satisfied—Jeremiah 31:14

_____ is saved—Ephesians 2:8

_____ is sealed by God with His Holy Spirit—Ephesians
1:13

_____ is seated with Him—Ephesians 2:6

_____ is secure—Deuteronomy 33:12

_____ is sent—John 20:21

_____ is set free—John 8:31–32, 36

_____ is sharing Christ's inheritance—Romans 8:17

_____ is sharing His glory—John 17:22, 24

_____ is one of His sheep—Psalm 23:1

_____ is sheltered—Psalm 91:1

_____ is shielded—Psalm 91:4

_____ is a slave to righteousness—Romans 6:18

_____ is a son of God—Romans 8:14

_____ is stable—Isaiah 33:6

_____ is standing in His grace—Romans 5:2

_____ is standing firm in Christ—2 Corinthians 1:21

_____ has his steps established by the Lord—Psalm 37:23

_____ is strengthened in Him—Ephesians 3:16

Which of the preceeding verses do you have trouble identifying with? Will you ask God to help you with it?

_____

_____

_____

_____

_____

_____ is strong in the Lord—1 Corinthians 1:8

_____ is amply supplied—Philippians 4:18

_____ is sustained from birth—Psalm 71:6

_____ is a temple—1 Corinthians 3:16

_____ is thought about—Psalm 139:17–18

_____ is transferred into His Kingdom—Colossians 1:13

_____ is transformed—2 Corinthians 3:18

_____ is treasured—Psalm 83:3

_____ is triumphant—2 Corinthians 2:14

_____ is unafraid—Isaiah 44:2, 51:12

_____ is understood—Ephesians 1:8

_____ is united with Christ—Romans 6:5

_____ is upheld—Psalm 37:17

_____ is upright—Psalm 7:10

_____ is unblemished—Colossians 1:22

_____ has understanding—2 Timothy 2:7

_____ is useful for His glory—Isaiah 43:7

_____ is valuable—Luke 12:24

_____ lives in victory—1 Corinthians 15:57

_____ is walking in His light—1 John 1:7

Pick one of the previous verses to memorize. Write it out here, and begin the process of committing it to memory.

_____

_____

_____

_____

_____

_____ is a warrior—2 Corinthians 10:4

_____ is washed—Titus 3:5

_____ is watching for His return—Luke 12:37

_____ is weak, then becomes strong—2 Corinthians 12:10

_____ is welcome—Luke 11:9

_____ is being made whole—Mark 5:34

_____ puts on the whole armor of God—Ephesians 6:11

_____ is wise—Proverbs 2:6

_____ is His witness—Acts 1:8

_____ is His workmanship—Ephesians 2:10

_____ is not of this world—John 17:14

_____ is His worshipper—Psalm 95:6

_____ is worthy—Revelation 3:4

_____ is yielded to God—Romans 6:13

_____ is yoked with Jesus—Matthew 11:29

_____ is heaven bound, guaranteed—1 Peter 1:4

One of the enemy's primary goals is to get you to nullify the identity Christ has set in you. If you can begin to see yourself as God sees you, you will be well on the way to the freedom that you desire.

I pray that you will see yourself as He sees you.

CHAPTER 10

CLEANSING

PART 1

> Purge me with hyssop and I shall be clean, wash me and
> I shall be whiter than snow....Create in me a clean heart
> O God, and renew a steadfast spirit within me.
>   —Psalm 51:7, 9

Section Goals:

- To understand the avenues God uses to bring cleanliness into our lives.
- To be equipped to allow God to cleanse our minds, bodies, and spirits through the use of key spiritual disciplines.
- To memorize Psalm 51:7, 9.

GOD DESIRES FOR us to be clean in every area of our lives—sexually, physically, spiritually, emotionally, and in every other area that you can think of.

For so long, my life was defined by dark, dank, and unclean places, people, and things. I often tell the story of how I was addicted to porn store viewing booths. These were places were men did any and every unclean sexual act imaginable. They were environments where I was surrounded by unimaginable smells; quiet and unclean sexual acts; and sad, enslaved men.

You may not ever have visited one of these places, or maybe you have. But I think that we can agree that for most of us, homosexual acts never sat well with the pit of our stomachs. We know that we longed for something cleaner, something more substantial. And this is the state of being that God wants us to attain and longs for us to experience. By His very nature, He is clean and wants us to know what it is like to feel clean too.

There are 2 aspects of cleansing that I want you to recognize: cleansing through the blood of Jesus and cleansing through confession.

CLEANSING THROUGH THE BLOOD OF JESUS CHRIST

Now I know that might sound sick. But just hear me out. The first and most powerful way that God cleanses us from sin is through the shed blood of Jesus Christ. His death on our behalf and the blood He shed are what paid the cost of our sins and what takes them away, leaving us guiltless in the eyes of God.

Let's look at Isaiah 53:3–10:

> He is despised and rejected by men,
> A Man of sorrows and acquainted with grief.

And we hid, as it were, our faces from Him;
He was despised, and we did not esteem Him.
Surely He has borne our griefs
And carried our sorrows;
Yet we esteemed Him stricken,
Smitten by God, and afflicted.
But He was wounded for our transgressions,
He was bruised for our iniquities;
The chastisement for our peace was upon Him,
And by His stripes we are healed.
All we like sheep have gone astray;
We have turned, every one, to his own way;
And the LORD has laid on Him the iniquity of us all.
He was oppressed and He was afflicted,
Yet He opened not His mouth;
He was led as a lamb to the slaughter,
And as a sheep before its shearers is silent,
So He opened not His mouth.
He was taken from prison and from judgment,
And who will declare His generation?
For He was cut off from the land of the living;
For the transgressions of My people He was stricken.
And they made His grave with the wicked—
But with the rich at His death,
Because He had done no violence,
Nor was any deceit in His mouth.
Yet it pleased the LORD to bruise Him;
He has put Him to grief.
When You make His soul an offering for sin,
He shall see His seed, He shall prolong His days,
And the pleasure of the LORD shall prosper in His hand.

This prophecy is commonly known as a *messianic prophecy*—one that is foretelling the coming of a Messiah who will suffer for the sake of His people, taking their sins upon Himself. Christians believe that this was fulfilled in the person of Jesus Christ when He was crucified, as told about in the New Testament.

Look at the following verses from the New Testament and complete the corresponding exercises:

1. Ephesians 1:7
    What are the two things that this verse says we have?
    _____ through His _____ and the _____ of sins

2. Matthew 26:27–28: "Then He took the cup, and gave thanks, and gave it to them, saying, 'Drink from it, all of you. For this is My blood of the new covenant, which is shed for many for the remission of sins.'"
    Circle the words "My blood" and "which is shed for many for the remission of sins." These words show us that we need to acknowledge the death Jesus experienced in order for judgment to be removed.

So from these verses, can you see that the goal that Christ had in going to the cross was to pay the price for the forgiveness of our sins? This is what takes away our guilt. This is what makes us clean. It is not our own righteousness, for Isaiah 64:6 says that "all our righteousnesses are like filthy rags…" But through Jesus' act of dying on the cross, He became our righteousness so that we might become righteous in God's eyes.

CLEANSING THROUGH CONFESSION

Read 2 Corinthians 5:21. The second way God washes us is through confession. While the blood of Christ washes us from the stain and guilt of sin, confession helps us to keep our daily sins always before the throne of God so that we can stay in fellowship with Him.

> If we confess our sins, He is faithful and just to forgive us our sins and to cleanse us from all unrighteousness.
> —1 John 1:9

This verse says that if we do something, God will do something.

What must we do?

_____

What will God do in return?

_____

_____

Confession is the process of bringing whatever wrong acts you have committed or your wrong motives for doing something before God and asking Him to forgive you for them. That's all. It is not always easy, and you may not always want to acknowledge that you did something wrong, but by the very act of confessing, you are telling God that you don't want to do the things you have been doing. You are saying that you're powerless and need Him to help you out.

First John chapter one is all about walking in fellowship with God. And confession of your sins will allow you to do just that. Verses 5–10 say, "…God is light and in Him is no darkness at all. If we say that we have fellowship with Him, and walk in darkness, we lie and do not practice the truth. But if we walk in the light as He is in the light, we have fellowship with one another, and the blood of Jesus Christ His Son cleanses us from all sin. If we say that we have no sin, we deceive ourselves, and the truth is not in us. If we confess our sins, He is faithful and just to forgive us our sins and to cleanse us from all unrighteousness. If we say that we have not sinned, we make Him a liar, and His word is not in us."

In addition to confessing to God, confession can be made to your Christian brothers and sisters. Now I am not telling you to spill all your business to every Christian you see, but I am saying that there will be times when talking with other like-minded Christians will bring healing into your life.

Look at James 5:16, which says, "Confess your trespasses to one another, and pray for one another, that you may be healed. The effective, fervent prayer of a righteous man avails much." There are going to be times when confession to someone else is appropriate. When done and received in the right spirit, this can bring healing. While my own church denomination does not practice confession in the same way Roman Catholics do, I do think that there are times when speaking to your pastor or another church leader is appropriate. They do not take precedence over God, but they can be a resource in helping you to bring about healing and cleanliness before God.

An example of confessing to others would be when I needed to confess to my wife about some acts of adultery I had committed. At the same time, I also confessed my mistakes to a mentor of mine who is also a committed Christian. Both confessions helped to bring healing into the situation and allowed me to learn better ways to deal with temptation.

In all this, I would be wary of one thing, though. Be careful of confessing or intimately conversing about your shortcomings with people outside of the faith. This would include homosexual friends or people who supported your homosexual lifestyle. This can lead to so many things— namely, temptation. I have fallen into this trap, and it led me to doubt and question the miracles I have seen God perform.

Personal Space

Read the first chapter of 1John. What is it telling you? Is there anything that you need to bring to God and confess? If so, you can take the time to do so now.

_____

_____

_____

_____

_____

_____

_____

_____

_____

_____

_____

For more of the Bible's teaching on confession, I suggest reading Proverbs 28:13 and Psalm 32:5.

I sincerely pray that you see how God desires for you to live holy, clean, and righteous in His sight. He says in 1 Peter 1:15–16, "But as He who called you is holy, you also be holy in all your conduct because it is written 'Be holy, for I am holy.'" He wants to see you succeed; He wants to see you overcome. The book of Genesis says that you were made in His image (Genesis 1:27), so wouldn't He want you to be like Him? Clean and holy?

Part 2

However, this kind does not go out except by prayer and fasting.

—Matthew 17:21

Section Goals:

- To learn spiritual disciplines that will help you to remain on the road towards sexual purity.
- To memorize Matthew 17:21.

We serve a God who longs to see us healthy and whole. We have already talked about how part of that health comes from cleanliness in His eyes. Homosexuality has stained us, and God desires for us to allow Him to wash us from it as we execute some spiritual disciplines in our lives.

As we saw in our discussion of confession, daily presentation of our bodies, minds, souls, and spirits to God is necessary for cleanliness. But the practice of homosexuality has left some marks on all of those things. There are often reminders of the homosexual life left in our minds and spirits that will lead us to temptation if we don't learn to wash them away.

On a practical level, I know that for me, one of those stains happens to be fantasy and memories. If I try hard enough (and often when I am not trying at all), I can recall acts and situations I participated in over fifteen years ago with amazing clarity. And when I don't check them through the use of a spiritual discipline, they can lead me to masturbation, or even worse, fornication. There is even cologne that I used to like to wear because it smelled like someone I was with. To this day I can recognize that scent any and everywhere. I had to ask God not only to help me kill my lust for it, but also to keep me as far away from it as possible.

I know that for many of you, it is the same. There are things, such as memories, pictures, and hungers and feelings for people, that will lead you right back to living as a homosexual if you linger on them. While we will talk more about this in the next section, I want you to know that God has given us some practices that can help us to clean all of this junk out of our lives.

Personal Space

Take a moment to assess some of the "ties" you have to homosexuality. They can be people, things, mementos from past relationships, erotic/pornographic movies, pictures, colognes, etc. List them here. In the next section, we will return to this list for another use.

_____

_____

_____

_____

_____

_____

_____

_____

In his book *The Life You've Always Wanted*[2], John Ortberg defines a spiritual discipline as: "Any activity that can help me gain power to live life as Jesus taught and modeled it." Isn't this our goal? To live life as Jesus taught and modeled? We want to serve Him, even in our sexuality. So it would be logical to assume that He would be happy to see us practicing anything that would allow us to do so.

I think that Ortberg's quote is a good definition of what I am going to talk with you about, namely certain things you can do to help you to 1) know Jesus more intimately and 2) remain walking in freedom from homosexuality.

I am sure you are excited to know what these activities are. I am excited to tell you! But first, I want to share three things that Ortberg says spiritual disciplines are NOT. I will list each point in his words and then expand upon his thoughts:

1. **"Spiritual disciplines are not a barometer of spirituality."** Your relationship with God is not defined by how much you pray or by how much you attend church. And a person who does these things more than you is not necessarily more spiritual than you. Don't feel condemned because you may do some of these things less frequently than others, because quite frankly, you can practice these disciplines every minute of every day, but if your motives are not right, you might not be any closer to God than when you started.

2. **"Spiritual disciplines are not necessarily unpleasant."** There are plenty of things that you can do to

enrich your relationship with God and to help you model your life after Christ that are not unpleasant. Serving the Lord can be a joy, don't think that you have to live like a monk in order to practice a spiritual discipline.

3. **"Spiritual disciplines are not a way to earn favor with God."** Please don't go to God in prayer and tell Him that I said that praying nine times a day should get you into heaven. I didn't say that! You cannot earn God's mercy or grace or gift of eternal life. You can't even earn freedom from homosexuality. They are all gifts. God is not an employer; He is a Father. Nothing we can do earns His favor. He gives it freely.

Now that we know what spiritual disciplines are not, we can enjoy their practice. Here's one more quote from Ortberg:

> "Following Jesus simply means learning from him how to arrange my life around activities that enable me to live in the fruit of the Spirit" (page 44).

That is the best definition I have come across regarding what it means to be a Christian, what it means to leave homosexuality, and what it means to practice a spiritual discipline.

So, without further ado, let me explain the four spiritual disciplines I have come to practice most frequently: prayer, fasting, Bible reading, and praising the Lord. All four help me to know what God expects of me, remind me of sin that I need to bring before Him, prompt me to ask Him for protection from temptation, and encourage me to simply let Him know that I appreciate all He does. I believe that all four disciplines are biblical. Let me tell you why.

Prayer and Fasting

Prayer and fasting go hand in hand, though I would say that prayer takes priority.

What is prayer? In my opinion, prayer is nothing more than a conversation with God—plain and simple. We can make it out to be something high and holy, but in reality, all you are doing is talking to Him and then letting Him talk back.

The reason prayer is vitally important to your freedom is because God is going to have to be your lifeline, your all in all. And in any relationship, we know that frequent, effective communication is the key to growth. Your relationship with Christ is no different. You are going to have to talk with Him, listen to Him, explain how you are feeling, lean on Him for comfort, and ask Him for help. There is no way of getting around it.

Let's look at what the Bible says about prayer. How do the truths in the following passages apply in practical and personal ways to your life and your struggles?

1. Praying for something can cause things to happen in your life and the lives of others. See Matthew 18:18–19.

_____

_____

2. Prayer will cause God to listen to what you have to say. See Psalm 141:1–2.

3. Prayer can be an avenue that brings peace into your life. See Philippians 4:6–7.

4. If you pray in the right spirit, God will reward you openly. See Matthew 5:14–16.

5. Prayers should be asked in the name of Jesus Christ. See John 16:23–24.

6. Prayer should accept the will of God, in whatever form it may come. See Luke 11:2.

_____

_____

7. In prayer, our sins can be forgiven if we confess them. See 1 John 1:9.

_____

_____

_____

It is vitally important to see that prayer is our direct connection to God. Through it, He can reveal areas in us that need to be exposed. Yet I do recognize this: Oftentimes, we have absolutely no idea what to say in prayer. That is why I offer three practices in prayer that can help:

1. **Pray God's Word**: Simply using Scripture as a starting point for prayer is a great way of not only getting the ball started, but also of knowing that your prayer is in God's will. We can often pray with wrong motives or ask for things that God does not desire for us. But if we take a portion of Scripture and use the words in our prayers, we know that we are praying the right way, as long as we pray in the right spirit and context of what the scripture is saying. This is because it is God's Word and He has to honor it. I mean, He said it! He, through men led by the Holy Spirit, wrote it down! And it is all the truth. So pray His words and promises back to Him, and see if He doesn't grant you an answer. Try starting with the Psalms; they are the prayers and emotions of men

who were trying to get closer to God, just as you are.

2. **Depend on the Holy Spirit to guide your prayers:** Read Romans 8:26. It tells us that oftentimes we do not know what to pray, so the Holy Spirit takes the groanings and moanings that we offer and makes intercession with God on our behalf.

3. **Journal:** I encourage you to journal often. It is a very therapeutic way of not only recording your prayers but also of getting a lot of feelings and emotions out in a way that you might not normally do. Writing can be good for the soul.

Now, what is fasting? Fasting is the act of going without physical food for an appointed amount of time. Biblically speaking, it is to abstain from food for the purposes of spending time with God for a specific reason.

Fasting can lead to cleansing because of the following benefits:

1. Fasting can allow for deliverance from some types of evil (Matthew 17:14 –21).

2. Fasting can petition God for answers to prayer.

3. Fasting can help you to overcome sexual addiction and bondage (Isaiah 58:6).

4. Fasting can help you bring your flesh into subjection/control (1 Corinthians 9:27).

The reason that I think that fasting is appropriate for men leaving homosexuality is this: It offers the opportunity to replace physical hungers with spiritual ones. In other words, it allows us to control the flesh.

I fast because I recognize that my hunger for sexual intimacy with men can be very strong. We all know that hungers can cause very strong convictions in us. Because of this, I like to "kill" my homosexual hungers and replace them with hungers for God.

In the book of Isaiah, God is speaking about the types of fasts that He approves of.

Isaiah 58:6 says, "Is this not the fast that I have chosen: To loose the bonds of wickedness, to undo the heavy burdens, to let the oppressed go free and that you break every yoke?"

According to Isaiah 58 verse 6, what are the four reasons God gives for a fast?

1. _____

2. _____

3. _____

4. _____

Homosexuality has been all of those things in my life. It has been a bond of wickedness, a heavy burden, an oppression, and a yoke. And I think that I am safe in assuming that if you are going through this journey with me, it has been those things to you also.

Let me offer two cautionary notes regarding fasting. They are very important, so please pay attention.

- **Fasting is not a requirement.** I am not saying in any way that fasting is required if you want to find salvation and freedom. While I think that evidence could be supplied that shows that the early church fasted frequently, I cannot find evidence that says that it is a requirement for freedom. Your belief in Christ is that requirement.

- **If you have a medical condition, you should contact your physician before attempting any type of fast.** I do not believe that God would ask you to put yourself in harm's way in order to fast. If you feel led to fast, consult a doctor first, or choose a partial, diet-restricting fast instead of a full-blown fast with no food or water.

Let me also offer a few pointers about how to fast:

- Fasting is always accompanied by prayer. In the Bible, we see that we can pray without fasting, but if we fast, we must spend time in prayer. This should be your main spiritual activity while you fast.

- Choose what you're going to fast from and the length of your fast ahead of time: fasting is a vow that you make to God for a specific time period. Whether it is for one hour or one week, a fast from a certain food or from all foods in general, make sure that you intend to adhere to your commitment.

- Do not try to manipulate God in your fast. When you fast, you are asking God to fill you up with strength and more of His will. But do not think that because you are fasting, God is obligated to comply. This is not the case.

- When you fast, do not fast for public recognition. This time is to be spent between you and God. As you fast, go about your day as if nothing is going on. See Matthew 6:16–18.

If you would like more information about fasting, I recommend the book *Fasting for Spiritual Breakthrough*[3] by Elmer L. Towns. It covers the topic at length and gives a lot of practical tips to get you started.

Because this can be a slightly controversial topic, I will simply say this about fasting: It is wonderful to feel that my physical hungers for men are decreasing as I bring them under subjection and fill myself up with more of the Word and of God. Fasting may not be for everyone, but it definitely has helped me to control my will and trade it for the will of God.

Bible Reading

Simply put, I believe that in order to know what it is that God expects of us, we have to read our Bibles. It's that simple. The Bible is God's instruction book to man. It is His love letter to us. Read it in order to find direction for your life and to be reminded of what He has done for us and how much He loves us. In particular, read Psalm 119. It tells us how important God's Word is to our well-being.

Praise

Praise is simply adoring God. That's all. When you praise God, what you are doing is giving God the glory in your life, telling Him how awesome and how majestic and how *great* He is. Praising God in hard times can keep you sane. It can help you to keep on course and to keep your eyes locked on Christ instead of on the man sitting next to you. It can help you to take your eyes off of all the junk inside of you—like the lust, obsessions, and impure thoughts about other men—and make you consider all of the great things that God has done in your life. This will slowly push the unclean stuff out as the clean, pure thoughts of God come rushing in.

No one can teach you how to praise the Lord. It is purely personal. But what I can do is give you an example from the Bible of what some men did to praise the Lord and what happened as a result. Here is the story from Acts 16:25–26:

> And at midnight Paul and Silas prayed, and sang praises unto God: and the prisoners heard them. And suddenly there was a great earthquake, so that the foundations of the prison were shaken: and immediately all the doors were opened, and every one's bands were loosed.

What were Paul and Silas doing prior to the earthquake?

_____

_____

That's right. They were praying and singing praises unto God. They were exalting Him, even as they sat in jail. And what was the result? An earthquake and the loosening of their shackles, that's what.

The story goes onto say that the jailer was so overtaken with the Spirit of God and Paul and Silas' preaching of the gospel to him that he let them go free.

In my spiritual imagination, I believe that if you begin to praise God in whatever way you know how, He will loosen your shackles and let you go free to walk in victory. It just takes your recognizing that God is the source of all there is and that He is worthy of adoration and worship.

In some charismatic churches, praise takes the form of dancing, shouting, singing, handclapping, upraised hands, exuberant music, and loud worship, as well as quiet states of awe, kneeling in the presence of God, and lying prostrate (face down) in worship. You can do these things as you worship alone, or your worship can be as simple as lifting your eyes to the heavens with a smile on your face. In whatever ways you feel most comfortable praising God, don't let anyone stop you. Get your praise on.

Personal Space

Here are some more verses about praise. Pick one, and make it personal in a journaled prayer.

Isaiah 43:21
1 Peter 2:9
Psalm 47
Psalm 34:1
Psalm 50:23

_____

_____

_____

_____

_____

_____

_____

_____

_____

_____

_____

I pray that you will find God in these disciplines and that you will gain more freedom as you learn more of His ways.

PART 3

> But put on the Lord Jesus Christ, and make no provision
> for the flesh, to fulfill its lusts.
>
> —Romans 13:14

Section Goal:

- To understand that in order to remain free and clean, you must destroy everything that would lead you to fall.
- To memorize Romans 13:14.

Let's get to the point. If you are not willing to clean every single thing out of your life that has any connection to homosexuality, you will never walk in total freedom. I know that this is a hard concept to grasp. I know that it hurts to think that you are going to have to cut off every avenue, every single reminder of homosexuality that you can tangibly take part in. But I assure you that if you do, God will honor your desire to be pure and clean in His eyes.

I had *a lot* of trouble with this. Some of the things that I cut off access to, I loved very much. I am going to be frank with you. It is going to hurt. You will possibly doubt God. You might want to give up on this Christianity thing all together. You will want to yell and scream at God and tell Him how unfair this is.

Please hang in there! The pain is worth it. When you come out of the fire and out of this test, you will be like pure gold in the eyes of God (Job 23:10). Now, before we go any further, I want you to stop and pray.

Personal Space

Please take the time to pray and ask God for strength for this endeavor. You are about to enter into some serious spiritual warfare, and you are going to need Him.

_____

_____

_____

_____

_____

_____

OK. Let's see what the Scriptures have to say about cutting off access to the things that would cause you to sin. Matthew 5:29–30 says, "If your right eye causes you to sin, pluck it out and cast it from you; for it is more profitable for you that one of your members perish, than for your whole body to be cast into hell. And if your right hand causes you to sin, cut it off and cast it from you; for it is more profitable for you that one of your members perish, than for your whole body to be cast into hell."

Think of the tendency to sin as an equation:

RESOURCES to Sin + OPPORTUNITY=DEATH

These words of Jesus are not telling you actually to go out and gouge out your eyes. But what they are doing is telling you to cut anything out of your life that will cause you to sin. *Anything*. Because as we can see in our equation, the RESOURCES to sin coupled with the OPPORTUNITY to use them will lead you right down the road to DEATH—both a spiritual death, and an eternal visit to hell if you don't forsake your sin and aren't in Christ.

It is better for you to go without some so-called pleasures now than to be eternally separated from God. I don't regret some of the things that I have cut off. After forsaking a lot of them, I found that most didn't give any long-term satisfaction anyway. The fantasy world that porn and anonymous gay sex offers doesn't last; later on, you will have to return to it to get another fix.

Let's look again at our opening verse: "But put on the Lord Jesus Christ, and make no provision for the flesh to fulfill its lusts" (Romans 13:14). This verse doesn't say you can make a few provisions. It doesn't say that an occasional trip to your porn stash or a midnight visit to your "ex" is OK. It doesn't say that you can attend an occasional gay pride meeting with your old friends or frequent a gay bar once in awhile. It says, *"Make no provision for the flesh."* God doesn't say you can sin once in a while. He told the woman who was accused of adultery to "...go and sin *no* more" (John 8:11, emphasis my own).

Hebrews 12:1, in the NLT says, "Therefore, since we are surrounded by such a huge crowd of witnesses to the life of faith, let us strip off every weight that slows us down, especially the sin that so easily trips us up. And let us run with endurance the race God has set before us." Like this verse says, we have so many examples of people in the Bible, witnesses to the faith, that we should be encouraged to run this race of freedom from homosexuality. So, because of their examples, this verse shows us the two things we need to do:

What are they? Fill in the blanks:

- strip off every _____
- especially the _____ that so easily _____
  _____.

You are going to have to rid yourself of everything that can hold you back. Here is a list of some of the things that I had to rid myself of:

- *Porn* in all its forms: magazines, videos, emails, unfiltered internet access, video clips, DVDs, CDs, and others.
- *Erotic movies and television*: Even though some movies and television shows are not pornographic, they can still portray homosexual or sexual themes in general. I needed to get rid of a lot of them.
- *An entire state in the United States of America*: Eventually, I had to accept the fact that I had too many ties to relationships and people in the state where I was born and raised. So I moved away. Temptation was everywhere, and I knew that for me, relocation was necessary to break some ties.
- *People unwilling to support my walk of freedom*: There were certain friends and acquaintances, both homo- and heterosexual, that I needed to limit, if

not eradicate, contact with for various reasons. I severed some homosexual friendships because they were unwilling to support me in my new lifestyle. I severed some heterosexual relationships for the same reason. Christ said that the cost of discipleship is taking up our crosses and following Him (Matthew 16:24). Sometimes that means losing friendships.

- Pieces of *clothing ands other objects*: There were some things in my wardrobe that gave my appearance a homosexual quality that needed to be destroyed. I wanted nothing to do with anything that made it look as if I still participated in the gay lifestyle.

- Access to *cash*: Especially after marriage, I had to limit my access to cash, because it was very tempting for me to enter a viewing booth with a pocketful of cash to spend. But if I didn't have access to cash and only an ATM or debit card, I could be held accountable by my wife or another accountability partner.

You may say that some of these things seem unreasonable, but for me they were necessary. While I think that there are going to be differences in each of us regarding the things that connect us to homosexuality, there are things that are obvious: porn, access to anonymous sex, and access to monogamous homosexual relationships, among others.

Your list may contain different things than mine. I can give you some suggestions, but make sure that in our next exercise, you are honest with what really ties you to your homosexual past.

Here are some suggestions of things that may be tying you to your homosexual past:

- Porn in all its forms.
- Erotic or homosexual entertainment: television, movies, novels, jokes.
- Romantic homosexual relationships.
- Gifts and mementos from past homosexual relationships.
- Gay pride literature.
- Unfiltered Internet access.
- A job that promotes or influences your homosexual past.
- Communities of friends who are unwilling to support you or who try to draw you back to the lifestyle.

Now there is nothing wrong with making the purging of these things from your life a memorable event. It can even be fun! I know, I know, that may be pushing it a little, but just hear me out.

One of the ministries I was a part of suggested having a burn/demolition party. Make sure you do it in a safe and legal way and place, but burning all of your porn or items can be very therapeutic. I did this with my stash of porn, pictures, and other stuff, and man, was it fun! To watch all of that stuff burn was like watching a part of my life that I hated be totally wiped away.

If you're married, another therapeutic thing that you can do is invite your spouse to the party. Use her as support, and watch your relationship become closer as you get further away from all of the stuff that holds you back.

Now it's your turn for assessment.

Personal Space

In the last section, you made a list of the "ties" that you have or had to homosexuality. Here, you can repeat that list, but take it a step further by listing ways in which you plan to eradicate these things from your life.

_____

_____

_____

_____

_____

_____

_____

_____

_____

_____

_____

_____

_____

_____

Some Advice

- Breaking relationships with friends who may still be in the lifestyle can be hard. You may find that there are some friends who, even unknowingly, are avenues for you to be around homosexual temptation or other sexual impurities. But if they are truly your friends, they will still be there when you tell them you can't participate in any homosexual activities, and they will encourage you to pursue God. If they're aren't your friends, now is the time for you to find out. There may come a time when you are strong enough to be around them and not succumb to homosexual activity, but that may only come after some time, if ever.

- Wiping these things out of your life is going to be hard if you're not filling the spaces up with something else. Now is the time for you to pursue Christian friendships. Stay involved in building clean relationships through church and other avenues. You will see that as you focus on other things, you will mourn the loss of these ties less and less. Hebrews 12:1–2 tells us to "strip off *every* weight that slows us down" by *"keeping our eyes on Jesus*, the champion who initiates and perfects our faith. Because of the joy awaiting him, he endured the cross, disregarding its shame. Now he is seated in the place of honor beside God's throne" (NLT, emphasis my own).

I pray that you will gain the confidence and strength to recognize and destroy everything that keeps you bound to homosexuality. There is a reward waiting for you, and I pray that you will obtain it.

CHAPTER 11

DISCIPLESHIP AND ACCOUNTABILITY

Iron sharpens iron, so one man sharpens another.

—Proverbs 27:17

Section Goals:

- To understand that living in community and being discipled by another man is crucial to maintaining freedom.

- To understand that being accountable to another person for your actions is necessary for life and will bring added peace and protection in the pursuit of freedom from homosexuality.

- To memorize Proverbs 27:17.

A S WE CONSTANTLY try to get closer to God in order to get farther away from the lives we hate, we have to be willing to undergo certain tangible changes in our daily lives. It's as if we have been given a diagnosis for a medical condition and the doctor says that we have to do certain things every day in order to maintain our health. As I have said before, I do not claim to have the secret formula for your healing, but I do believe God does. I also believe that He has given us access to certain people and certain things that are there to help us stay on the right path.

In this section, we will look at the practices of discipleship and accountability. Without both in our lives, I believe that the journey from meeting your same-sex needs to a lifestyle of purity in God's eyes will be hard and lonely, if not impossible.

BEING DISCIPLED

In our first section goal, you see that I used a word that is slightly more forceful than the similar word I used in the second goal. Instead of the word "necessary," I used the word "crucial" in describing the topic of discipleship. This is because I do not believe that I would be alive today or on the road towards freedom if it had not been for someone mentoring me.

My mentor is a Christian man who is also living contrary to his sexual attraction to men. At a time when I knew the Lord but did not know if I could walk this journey alone, when I was ready to give up, the Lord placed this man in my life to be an encourager, a teacher, a brother, a friend, a confidant, a listening ear, and a chastiser. Without his constantly pointing me towards the cross, affirming my manhood, and telling me I am wrong when it's appropriate, my marriage would not be intact, my confidence and self-esteem would be nonexistent, and I probably would have succeeded at my suicide attempt. That is why I am here to tell you that it is absolutely *crucial* for you to pray for godly counsel to come into your life.

But instead of taking me at my word, let's look to the Word of God. Ecclesiastes 4:9–12 says, "Two are better than one, because they have a good reward for their labor. For if they fall, one will lift up his companion. But woe to him who is alone when he falls, for he has no one to help him up. Again, if two lie down together, they will keep warm; but how can one be warm alone? Though one may be overpowered by another, two can withstand him. And a threefold cord is not easily broken."

What do these verses say will happen if a person who has a companion falls?

_____

_____

This passage says that if one should fall, his companion will be able to lift him up. This is so utterly important for you. You have to realize that as you walk along this road to freedom, all the praying you can do, all the fasting and delighting in God's Word, all the cleansing and reading and such will only take you so far if you try to go at it alone.

The people who make up the church, the body of Christ, are meant to depend on one another. And as you daily forsake your past and walk away from friends and relationships and feelings that you have counted on for so long, you are going to get extremely lonely and extremely discouraged if there is no one tangible for you to talk to.

Galatians 6:2 tells us, "Bear one another's burdens, and so fulfill the law of Christ." God wants us to walk this journey *together*.

We are all members of the body of Christ. And God has given each one of us a gift to execute in ministry to each other (Romans 12:5–6). We have to love each other; we have to depend on each other. This is the way Christian, brotherly love was made to function. If we don't do this, the church will suffer, and your journey out of homosexuality will be lonely.

I tried to live this life without the church. I tried to walk in freedom on my own, not disclosing my struggles with my sexuality to anyone and living extremely sheltered. It was then that I fell into adultery because I had no one to pray with when I was struggling and no one to talk to when I was lonely. Each member of the body of Christ *has* to connect itself in confession, encouragement, and the worship or God. This life doesn't work without it.

I know that this can be scary. I know that talking about your life with men who may not feel the way you do and don't understand your feelings is the last thing you want to do. I often still don't want to do it. But it's necessary for growth.

Here are some tips for starting out:

- Start off slow. Start by possibly becoming involved in a small group at church, preferably one with men your age or a little older. Don't feel like you have to spill everything the minute you meet someone, but slowly acclimate yourself to being around other people. There is nothing that says that just because you are around other men, you have to talk about your past. Let it come up in appropriate situations if the Spirit leads you. And if it doesn't, don't feel like you have to talk about it all the time. There is plenty of encouragement that can be found that doesn't have to make you feel different or like an outcast.

- There are a plethora of Internet ministries available for men who may be struggling with same-sex attraction. If you have access to the Internet, consider joining in on discussion boards or other community building activities that are being used to promote freedom from homosexuality. Visit our Web site at www.thesearchforfreedom.org, or visit any of the ministries listed in Appendix B of this book.

- Exodus International is a referral agency for ministries that have support groups, mentorship programs, live-in ministries, and counseling agencies in your area. Log onto their Web site at www.exodus-international. org to find a ministry near you.

- If you aren't a member of one already, join a Bible-believing church where the Bible is taught and Christ is exalted. In a community of believers, you can find sound teaching as well as fellowship with other believers.

- Pray. I believe that if you ask God for a mentor and friend, He will send you one.

- Know your limitations. As you first begin to walk in freedom, be careful of being alone with other men who may be struggling, either in public, on the phone, or on the Internet. Stick to group settings until you feel you can venture out. But even then, keep your eyes on God and remain accountable to someone.

Two of the greatest examples of discipleship in the Bible are first, Jesus and His twelve disciples, and second, Paul and Timothy. Jesus' main goals with the disciples were to not only to equip them for ministry after He was gone but also to teach and guide them while He was still around. At one point, He even called them His friends because they had entered into a point in their relationship where they had become extremely close (John 15:15–17).

Paul and Timothy were also in a mentor/disciple relationship. Paul was the elder and Timothy a young man who was beginning to lead a life of ministry. In his letter to Timothy, Paul encouraged and equipped him to go forward in life and ministry. (Read the books of 1 and 2 Timothy.)

I met my mentor through an online Bible study. Even though we have a close relationship today that is able to stand being alone together (even our wives hang out and fellowship together!), we recognize that we are not supposed to leave any room for temptation to set in, so we both frequently engage in groups at church and online. I have come to depend on him in hard times, and we both learn so much from each other. I consider our Christian relationship to be of great value in my life.

Personal Space

Where are you at with this concept? Do you see that discipleship and being mentored are beneficial to your freedom? What steps can you take to initiate being discipled or to begin looking for a mentor?

_____

_____

_____

_____

_____

_____

_____

_____

_____

BECOMING ACCOUNTABLE

Accountability is very similar to discipleship, but it has some differences that I think add substance to our walk of freedom.

"Accountability" is defined as the state of being accountable—under obligation or willing to accept responsibility for—something or someone. In our search for freedom, being held accountable for our actions can curb some of the mistakes or submissions to sin that we might find ourselves making.

In my relationship with my mentor, it is good to know that I have someone looking out for my best interests. My mentor often has keen insights into things in my life that may be holding me back from walking in freedom. He often asks me if something I am doing is causing me pain or points out things that I may not see that are linking me to my past.

While I was going to my previous church, my pastor would point out these types of things, always doing it in a spirit of love. For example, I had grown up with a habit of tying my sweaters around my waist as a way of keeping them with me. The thing I did not realize was that this was drawing attention to a feminine stride that I had and was making men (who I didn't know were looking at the time) focus on my rear. My pastor pointed this out, and together, we were able to change this style of dress.

Now, was this type of dress harmless? For some it is. Is it a sin to wear a sweater that way? No. But the attention it was bringing me was an avenue to possible temptation. So for me, it was something that needed to be changed. But without that type of relationship of accountability, I may never have seen it.

The Bible says, "Brethren, if a man is overtaken in a trespass, you who are spiritual restore such a one in a spirit of gentleness, considering yourself lest you also be tempted. Bear one another's burdens and so fulfill the law of Christ" (Galatians 6:1). Relationships of accountability are supposed to help believers who may be faltering in an area either to come back to the Lord after confessing sin or to see areas of temptation before they fall. These relationships are also supposed to encourage and support. The Bible says that we are to "rejoice with those who rejoice" (Romans 12:15).

Personal Space

Here are some more Scripture references on the topic of accountability. Read them and try to figure out what God is saying to you.

Hebrews 10:23–25

_____

_____

_____

_____

Proverbs 28:13

_____

_____

_____

_____

Hebrews 3:13

_____

_____

_____

_____

Some Tips for Accountability Relationships

- If you are married, your first and most important accountability partner should be your spouse. She is your helper and friend, and if you are still practicing sin or committing adultery, you have an obligation to let her know, especially as you may be putting her health at risk for catching a sexually transmitted disease.

- Accountability partners are not Christ. You are not to use them as a crutch, looking to them to solve every one of your problems. They are there to encourage, equip, and spiritually discern temptations that you may not see.

- When you enter an accountability relationship, you are granting your partner permission to ask all the hard questions. Now is not the time to get squeamish. Their job is to encourage you to get into the Word, to ask you if you have been viewing porn or cruising bars, etc. This person is not always going to function as a friend; sometimes it takes tough love to get someone to see areas that need help.

- You grant your accountability partner permission into the intimate parts of your life. This doesn't mean that you divulge any and everything, but it does call for openness, honesty, and transparency.

- The best accountability partnerships happen when both parties are active participants. Everyone struggles with something. So that you don't feel like a patient going to a shrink, seek out a partner who is humble enough to make communication and accountability a two-way street.

My accountability partners are my wife and my mentor. Both have my permission to ask whatever they may feel led to ask. It is because of these relationships that I have dodged a whole lot of sinful mistakes.

In the definition of accountability, I stated that we can be held accountable to people or things. I think that one of the best things that can hold us accountable in the age of the World Wide Web is a good Internet filtering system.

With the size of the porn industry being what it is today and with it being readily available on the Internet, it is virtually impossible not to come across porn. Installing an Internet filter, blocking all porn and erotic material on your computer, will keep you temptation free while roaming the 'Net. I used to spend hours upon hours, entire *days* searching for porn on the Internet. When I installed a filter on my computer, it made it virtually impossible to gain access to any, and it greatly reduced my temptation.

I can wholeheartedly recommend the Safe Eyes™ Internet filtering system. It is inexpensive, nonthreatening to your computer, and even has a tool that will send a report of every site you even *attempt* to view to an e-mail address or telephone number of your choice. This can enable you to have a report automatically sent to your accountability partner so that you guys can encourage each other for victories made or develop a game plan for you while you surf the 'Net. You can find Safe Eyes at www.safeeyes.com and in Appendix B of this book.

Only you know what your situation is. There may be other areas that you recognize you need to be held accountable for. As I mentioned before, for me, one of those was carrying cash. This was a temptation for me because it was easy to run into a viewing booth and drop ten bucks on an in-store movie without anyone knowing. So today, I carry only an ATM/debit card so that my wife can keep track of where money is being spent through our bank statements.

Personal Space

Who in your life may be a candidate to serve as an accountability partner for you? If you don't have any ideas, pray and ask God for someone. In what other areas of your life do you need accountability? Is it on the Internet? Is there some other area? Come up with a game plan for accountability in those areas.

_____

_____

_____

_____

_____

_____

I pray that God will send people into your life who will be there to encourage you and hold you accountable so that you can succeed on this journey.

CHAPTER 12

A HEALTHY SEXUALITY

"And the Lord God said, 'It is not good that man should be alone; I will make him a helper comparable to him.' Therefore a man shall leave his father and mother and be joined to his wife, and they shall become one flesh."

—Genesis 2:18, 24

Section Goals:

- To understand what a healthy sexuality looks like.
- To understand how marriage can help maintain freedom from homosexuality.
- To memorize Genesis 2:18, 24.

I NOW WANT TO talk with you about a very sensitive subject. Leaving homosexuality is going to be a very lonely road if a healthy sexuality isn't developed. I will do my best to salt all of my words with as much grace as possible.

Outside of being discipled and meeting the grace of God face to face, marriage and sexual intimacy with my wife has had the greatest influence over my long-term, substantial walk of freedom. I cannot think of something that I value more. The love, intimacy, and companionship that I found in marriage to a godly, God-fearing, God-seeking woman cannot be compared to any of the relationships that I fostered outside of the Word of God. And I sincerely believe that those same feelings of love, intimacy, and companionship can be yours, too.

I am totally aware that for some of us, there seems to be absolutely no attraction to the opposite sex. I happen to be fortunate enough to never have experienced the lack of those feelings; I was attracted to both sexes for as long as I can remember. But I do know men who do not desire homosexual feelings and yet they have no idea how to foster feelings for women. It can be a totally lonely existence, and I pray continually for men who may feel that way.

Whether or not you happen to be one of those men, I have to believe that it is possible for God to help you develop those feelings. Every time that I accepted God's Word at face value and believed in the plan that He has ordained for sexuality and life in general, I found that He makes good on His promises.

God's Word shows us that marriage, sexual intimacy, and biblical companionship are honorable in His eyes. He has already told us that one, homosexuality is not His plan for us, and two, sexual relationships are to be between a married man and woman. If that is the case, we have to believe that He will make it possible for us to positively function in a heterosexual relationship, even if we don't know how. Will it be easy? No. But I do think it is possible.

Let's examine what a healthy sexuality is, and let me give you my reasons for why I think that you can function in it. But before I do, let's have some personal space.

Personal Space

Take a minute and evaluate your attraction to the opposite sex. Do you have one? If so, do you think and believe that it can be strengthened? If you don't have one, why do you think this is so? More importantly than that, do you believe that God can help you develop one?

_____

_____

_____

_____

_____

_____

_____

_____

_____

_____

_____

I have no answer for the question of how to develop sexual feelings for the opposite sex if they do not exist. What I do know is this:

- James 1:17 says that every good gift comes from God, and Luke 11:9 says that if we ask God for things, He will supply them, according to His will. Shouldn't this be the same for our sexualities?

- Genesis 2:18 says, "And the Lord God said, 'It is not good that man should be alone; I will make him a helper comparable to him.'" God doesn't want you to be alone. He knows your need for companionship. Why would He allow you to be lonely and frustrated with a sexuality that you don't want and not give you the desire for a healthy sexual, intimate relationship if you ask Him for it?

- 1 Corinthians 7 talks a lot about marriage. One of the things it says is that if a man is unable to control his lusts, he should marry in order to stay pure before God. It also alludes to the fact that it is also OK to stay unmarried and celibate. I would venture to say that as hard is it may be, if a man is unable to develop a heterosexual orientation, he should remain unmarried. God will provide ways for Him to meet his same-sex intimacy needs appropriately and to control his lust.

WHAT IS MARRIAGE?

And the LORD God said, "It is not good that man should be alone; I will make him a helper *comparable* to him."

Out of the ground the LORD God formed every beast of the field and every bird of the air, and brought them to Adam to see what he would call them. And whatever Adam called each living creature, that was its name. So Adam gave names to all cattle, to the birds of the air, and to every beast of the field. But for Adam there was not found a helper comparable to him. And the LORD God caused a deep sleep to fall on Adam, and he slept; and He took one of his ribs, and closed up the flesh in its place. *Then the rib which the LORD God had taken from man He made into a woman, and He brought her to the man.* And Adam said: "This is now bone of my bones and flesh of my flesh; She shall be called Woman, because she was taken out of Man." *Therefore a man shall leave his father and mother and be joined to his wife, and they shall become one flesh.* And they were both naked, the man and his wife, and were not ashamed. (Genesis 2:18–25, emphases my own)

There are some key components of these verses that we need to understand. First, the word which is translated "comparable" is the Hebrew word *neged,* which means " an opposite part" or "a counterpart or mate." What does this mean in light of verse 18?

_____

_____

_____

_____

Adam had just been given the job of naming all of the animals on earth by God, but there was not a mate or comparable to be found by him. God recognized this and desired for Adam not to be lonely and to have a physical human partner who would fulfill all of the parts that were missing for Adam: social intimacy, physical intimacy (sex), and the reproduction of the race. In verses 23–25, we see God instituting marriage for Adam. In verse 23, where does Adam say that woman came from?

_____

Out of man. There is a part of every man on the face of the earth, a spiritual connection that attracts him to the opposite gender, because the opposite gender was, is, and always will be a part of him. Woman is the missing part of man. She not only provides help in daily living, but a physical, sexual, and spiritual intimacy that was ordained by God.

Before we even get to how this pertains to the homosexual struggle, we need to accept that the basis for natural sexual relationships and the overall institution of marriage functions as being between one man and one woman in God's eyes.

Personal Space

Where are you with this? Are you able to accept the fact that the union in which a positive sexuality is fostered is between a man and a woman?

_____

_____

_____

_____

_____

_____

_____

_____

_____

How Can Marriage and Freedom Go Hand in Hand?

Building sexual intimacy with a woman can be hard for a man who has sought it out from other men. Even though I myself have always been attracted to women as well as men, I know what it is like to desire that intimacy with a man even in the midst of finding it with my wife. That is why I am going to let you in on the two things that marriage is not, the culmination of which will bring me to another point:

- *Marriage is not a union with all of female kind.* It is intimacy on a spiritual, emotional, and physical level with one woman. I think that if we take the focus off of feeling like we have to be attracted to all of womankind and instead focus on growing in intimacy with our wives, we will be a lot better off.

168 • THE SEARCH FOR FREEDOM

Some of you may be thinking, "How can I think of marriage when I have no attraction for women?" That is a very good question, and to be honest, I don't have an answer that will flip a heterosexual switch in your emotions. All I can say is that through intense commitment to faith in God, I have seen men who struggle with homosexual feelings find women who are willing to marry them, fulfill their sexual needs, and minister to them as a wife. And in return, I have seen them develop a love so much stronger than in any homosexual relationship I have come across. On the flip side, I have also seen men who are able to keep themselves from sexual immorality while remaining single. But this comes in situations where the men have a very focused control over their bodies and their actions. Either way, I think that the most important thing is to seek God and either ask Him for the power to stay single and pure or to give you a woman who will be able to meet you in all areas of your life, sexually as well as otherwise.

- *Marriage is not a substitute for same gender intimacy*: As human beings, we have needs that have to be met and a desire to connect with both sexes; God simply says that your sexual needs are not to be met by the same gender. We are supposed to fellowship with, relate to, and be affirmed by other men, just not sexually. Our sexual needs are to be met by our opposite, the woman in our life we call "wife." She is there to fulfill those sexual desires and give us enough room to connect with other men in fellowship and comraderie.

Based on the following verse in **Personal Space**, we can see the basis for the previous two points. We also are able to see that when we practice a biblical sexuality within a marriage, marriage can be a *deterrent to sexual immorality*,

Personal Space

Record your feelings about the following verse: "But because of the temptation to sexual immorality, each man should have his own wife and each woman her own husband. The husband should give to his wife her conjugal rights, and likewise the wife to her husband" (1 Corinthians 7:2–3).

_____

_____

_____

_____

_____

_____

Next up, I am going to let you in on something that I usually keep very sacred: my own marriage.

Marriage for me has not been easy, but it has definitely been worth it, because it has helped me to do a number of things: stay pure before the Lord, love another person in the right way, and stay away from sexual immorality as much as possible. But I think instead of giving you cliché answers on marriage and healthy sexuality, it would be better if I illustrate to you how they have brought me closer to grace.

1. *Before marriage, I had no self control*: When I first accepted Christ, I was already in a relationship with the woman who would come to be my wife. I knew that if I told her about my past, there was the possibility of her leaving me. It just so happened that I gave my life to the Lord the same night that I told my would-be wife about my past, and in my prayer to Him I made a special request. Privately, I asked Him for a woman who would accept my past and look beyond it. I told Him that He most likely already knew that I was unable to remain celibate for any extended length of time, so if He wanted me to remain pure, I would at least need to have the possibility of marriage. Not only did He give me the possibility, He gave me the reality, a woman who looked beyond my past sexual activity and was willing to work with me, so to speak. My wife today is the woman who God sent not only for me to have a sexual outlet, but also to learn to love selflessly and unconditionally.

2. *In the bedroom, education is a part of the curriculum*: From the beginning of my marriage, I knew how to function in the bedroom. There was no problem in finding satisfaction in the physical act. But what was a problem was learning to be emotionally and spiritually intimate, not simply physically. Over time, through the practice of making a conscious effort to open up, intimacy with and an attraction to my wife multiplied a hundredfold. My wife took the time to work with me, to teach me how to allow myself to

like what women had to offer. She ministered to me on a physical, educational, and spiritual level. Even though this may sound sacrilegious, and I hope it isn't taken that way, our faith came into the room with us. She takes her role as a wife who is to meet her husband's physical needs seriously. Even when she knows that it is making me slightly uncomfortable, she kisses me and dotes on me to show me that her love is nothing unusual or something to dislike. She simply loves to fulfill my needs.

Let me say this again before we go on: education is key in the bedroom. You will have to find out what you do and do not like. In marriage, you have to learn to like things and you have to be an explorer of sorts. The Bible says that intimacy between a husband and wife is a good thing. Even if you have never experienced it, you may find that heterosexual sex feels better than you may have thought.

3. *In marriage, I was thrust into the role of head of household and member of the male community:* From the beginning, my wife set it in her head that she was going to put me into situations where I was going to have to learn what it meant to be a man. Not just in the macho sense, but in the biblical one. She made it absolutely clear that she expected me to lead the family. This included maintaining an income, leading spiritual affairs (such as prayer and family devotions), and setting an example of manhood for our son and daughter. She also made it clear that she would stand as my "comparable helper" or a "help

meet" for me (Genesis 2:18). This doesn't mean
that there are exclusive roles in gender or that we
practiced some kind of sexism, it was just that she
pushed me into leadership and stood next to me as
a companion. Finally, she makes it very clear that
not only am I supposed to find satisfaction in her,
but also that she is supposed to find it in me. That
means that I cannot simply deny her sex because I
feel like it. There are only two biblical reasons for
denying your spouse sex: for prayer and fasting.
Homosexual feelings for another man are not a valid
reason. This showed me that not only was she not
unhealthily focused on me, but also she was thinking
of herself. But even more than that, it meant that she
was worried about my sexuality as much as I was,
because she was doing what she could to help me
develop a healthy one.

4. *Marriage makes me think of someone other than myself:*
    On the road out of homosexuality, it can be very easy
    to think of no one outside of yourself; to think of
    how lonely you are, how pitiful you are, blah, blah,
    blah. But when I got married, I couldn't do that. I
    had a wife who was counting on me and later on a
    son who needed a father who set the right example.
    I knew that I had not only a spiritual and emotional
    responsibility to my wife but also a physical one. I
    couldn't deny her; it wasn't right. All of this made
    me think more about the road out of homosexuality
    rather than about the road in, even if I did sometimes
    desire to go back.

5. *Most importantly, marriage has shown me the true grace of God*: In the Christian world, "grace" is defined as the completely undeserved mercy of God. But I do not know if we realize just how deep or how wide or how big that grace is. I did not know the true definition of mercy or grace or the real brokenness of spirit over sin, until I committed adultery and was forgiven. Now, I am not saying that you need to commit adultery in order to experience forgiveness in marriage, because you don't. But I will say that if you are blessed enough to find a wife who will look past your faults, who will look past your homosexual feelings and love and respect you anyway, you will most definitely see the grace of God in full bloom. It will be so beautiful that you will feel completely broken in its presence and will not desire to tarnish it with adultery or fornication.

Once again, I do not know how you find a woman to love and trust and be attracted to if you do not have an attraction to women. But again, I do believe it is possible. I believe in a God who is big enough and powerful enough to open up the windows of heaven and bless you immensely if your heart is in the right place and if you are seeking Him. Pray and ask God for a change of heart, for a renewed attraction. If it is in His will for your life (and I believe it is), He will grant it to you. If His desire is for you to remain single and chaste, He will empower you to be able to do that also. Just seek Him.

Personal Space

Record your thoughts, feelings, frustrations, and questions about this lesson. When you're done, give them to God and let Him make sense of them all.

_____

_____

_____

_____

_____

_____

_____

_____

_____

_____

_____

_____

I pray for God's power in you. I pray that God will help you to see the value in heterosexual intimacy.

CHAPTER 13

A MESSAGE OF ENCOURAGEMENT FROM MY WIFE

This section is the greatest opportunity available to me to let you hear from the woman who is helping me become the man God has called me to be. I believe that I would not be in the place of freedom that I am today if it had not been for her, because she believed in my healing when I did not believe in it myself. She has borne shame and humiliation because of my actions, and I would be totally out of order if I did not allow her to be a part of the work we are doing here. Here is a message to you from her. There are no personal spaces in this section, but I do ask that you meditate on what she has to say.

THREE YEARS INTO our marriage, I decided that it was over. I was going to leave my husband. I had every right to; he had committed adultery. And not only had he committed adultery, but also he had committed it with another *man*. I was hurt, betrayed, and felt both used and abused. My number one reason was that "it wasn't fair." I did not deserve the treatment he was dishing out.

On that same day, I was forced to change my decision and stay. I say "forced" because as I was crying out to God and asking Him "why?" and "what did I do to deserve this?", telling Him over and over that this wasn't fair, very quietly, and I heard Him respond, "So?"

That response initially sounded cruel and unempathetic. But as I stayed in meditation, He allowed me to see that my marriage was a perfect example of His marriage to the world.

See, God is the Faithful One. He treats me right and loves me unconditionally. I am the one who is imperfect, the one who cheats on Him both subconsciously and consciously, always seeming to put other things before Him. Just as when we accept Jesus into our lives and become one with God, we enter into covenant with him, meaning that we enter into a loving, contractual agreement. He loves us unconditionally and in return for grace, mercy, forgiveness and much more, we promise him the same. I can recall times where I made promises to God and said I was going to do things for Him and never did. I decided to watch television instead of pray to Him, was afraid to say His name in front of certain people—the list goes on. Yet even still, God forgives me and still accepts me as His Bride.

Well, this is what God showed me all in one day: When my husband and I were married, we made a vow to each other that stated that only death would separate us. Those vows are no different than His covenant with us. I am imperfect and my husband is imperfect so we should expect to have flaws and weaknesses and to break promises. Just as God accepts us for who we are and says, "Come as you are," the bride says to the groom and the groom says to the bride the very same thing (Revelation 21:17).

This is what I said to my husband: "Come. Come to me as you are, and I will walk this journey towards freedom with you." I prayed with him, cried with him, sought the Lord with him, and bore his burdens. It all started with his opening up to me, telling me who he really was. Then I had to accept who he *was*, forgive him for what he *did*, and then be the woman he needed me to be. This was the process of reconciliation.

I share this to tell you that there is *hope*; that with the love of God your life does not have to be what it is. Six years later, my husband and I are still happily married, and we have three children. We have accepted each other's flaws, while having patience enough for God to work out the ones that hinder us from having a real relationship with one another. When I look at him, I not only see the man that I married, but also: I see the blood of Jesus. I see deliverance. I see the grace and power of God. I see life. I see a testimony. I see a man who is walking the road towards freedom!

As a woman and a wife, I want to pass on the best advice I can give you:

1. If you are in a relationship with a woman and you've committed homosexual acts behind her back, confide in her about your struggle. Tell her the truth; be honest. That was one thing I respected my husband for. The fact that he was honest with

me was his way of crying out for help; his way of telling me that he did not desire to live the lifestyle anymore. I was able to look at him not as a cheater but as a friend and as someone who needed my help. I am not telling you that she will definitely do as I did, but at least you can say you were open, honest, and repentant.

2. Ask for forgiveness. Once you have told her the truth, ask her for forgiveness. Ask her to forgive you for cheating, lying, deceiving, and not "keeping it real" between you. You also must ask God for forgiveness. (This, in fact, should come *first*, because once God forgives you, He will give you assurance that you are not condemned for your actions, whether or not your woman/wife forgives you.) And once you have asked for forgiveness, *let it go* (Philippians 3:13, 14)! Know that you are forgiven and that God does not hold it against you (Micah 7:19).

3. Seek help. Get an accountability person. This is the point where you need to show your woman/wife that you are sincere about changing your lifestyle. You will not be able to do it alone, because you yourself are the problem. You live in flesh, and your flesh is what desires to engage in sin. It is going to take a spiritually-grounded person to help you through your journey. Remember, it is the power of the Holy Spirit that changes the person from the inside out and helps you not to yield to temptation. So you want to find someone who has the power of the Holy Spirit working in him so he will be able to mentor you in spirit and in truth.

4. Build intimacy. If you are married or are in a
   relationship with a woman, remind yourself of why
   you married or are in the relationship with her. Do
   an assessment of what she really likes. Whatever it
   is, do it for her or give it to her (as long as God will
   find pleasure in it). I heard someone once say that
   INTIMACY stands for "in–to–me–you–see." Release
   your sexual desires onto her. (That is, if you are
   married. You don't want to leave one sin to enter
   into another—1 Corinthians 6:9–10.) Increase the
   frequency of having sex. Increase the frequency of
   alone time to hug. Talk, go out to eat, and engage in
   other "togetherness" activities. Immediately when
   you feel the urge or desire to look at, go after, or
   think about another person, that is the time to run
   to your wife and hold her, kiss her, or open yourself
   up to her. The more you are spending time with each
   other, the stronger the relationship becomes. And
   if you're with her then, you're not with someone or
   something else.

Finally, and most importantly, the best person to
be intimate with is God. He loves intimacy. He loves
it when someone spends time with Him, tries to get to
know Him, seeks His face and what He likes, and then
goes out of his or her way to please Him by giving Him
what He wants. God is able to fill that empty hole that
you've been filling up with your own lusts. God wants
to be close to you!

My prayer for you from the heart:

Father God, in the name of Jesus, I thank you for the opportunity to share with others how you have graced my husband and me with a powerful testimony. We wouldn't have it any other way. Through our struggles, we have learned to be closer and have realized the kind of love and power you have.

Lord, I pray for all the men who have had similar struggles to those of my husband. I pray that you will touch their hearts and let them know that they are still loved by you regardless of their past or their present because you have invested in their future. I ask that if there is a woman in their life, that you give her a spirit of forgiveness and strength to endure this journey with them. I pray for these men that you would provide for them a suitable replacement, that when they are tempted they can turn to someone or something that will satisfy their souls and bring pleasure unto you. I pray for whomever you have led to read these words, that the words will settle in their minds and in their hearts, that they may have hope, faith, and the "peace that surpasses all understanding."

Now Lord, if there is one who does not know you as his personal Lord and Savior, I ask that you use the Holy Spirit to guide him in the right direction, that he may believe in his heart and confess with his mouth that you came to this earth to die and were resurrected and that you will soon return to reunite for eternity with all who have accepted you. In Jesus' name I pray. Amen!

To God be the Glory, both now and forever in your life,
Dayona Ellis

CHAPTER 14

PRESS ON

Now unto Him who is able to keep you from falling, and to present you faultless before the presence of His glory with exceeding joy, To the only wise God our Savior, be glory and majesty, dominion and power, both now and ever. Amen.

—Jude 24, 25

AS WE END this written journey together, I want to tell you that I am proud of you. I know you are probably asking yourself how I could be proud of someone I never met, but I am telling you, it's possible. I am proud of you for two reasons. One, you put up with me for this long! And two, you love God enough to finish this book. Your reading of this final section shows that you want to know God in His fullness and serve Him with your sexuality. I believe that He is sitting on His throne with a humongous grin on His face, giddy with excitement over the life of freedom and holiness that you are embarking on. Be proud of yourself! You are doing what God wants you to do. Having God smile because of you is the greatest gift anyone can ever receive.

As we end, I want you to know that you can make it. If you get anything out of what I have said in these pages, get this: you can make it. As I said in the beginning, I am not a theologian or scholar. I am simply someone testifying to the goodness and power of God. The only thing I endeavor to do is encourage you. Your sexual appetites don't dictate whether or not God loves you. He does that regardless. But you have the opportunity to show Him that you love Him back by living the way He wants you to live.

As you step out in freedom, there are going to be people who tell you that homosexuals can't change. They are going to tell you that you are in denial, that you are sexually repressed. Don't believe them! Look them square in the face and smile, knowing that Jesus Himself was persecuted. How can you expect any less (John 15:20)?

We need you to stand up for what God has done in your life. That doesn't mean you have to tell everyone you pass on the street, but it means that we need you not to be ashamed of the Christ who is in you. He is working in you to make you holy. The gospel needs to be spread, and there are men who are feeling the way you and I have felt but don't know yet that they can be free. Find a way to tell them. Spread the message of this book. Your testimony of freedom benefits others who want to leave homosexuality as well as yourself. The book of Revelation says that they—the ones who had been accused all their lives by the devil, namely us—"overcame him by the blood of the Lamb and *the word of their testimony*" (Revelation 12:11, emphasis my own). Never stop testifying to the power of God to free captives. You will strengthen others as well as strengthen yourself.

Thank you for spending time with me. I hope you know that I pray for you constantly. I don't know your name, but I lift you up before Him always anyway. You are constantly on my mind. Know that someone is always praying for you.

Remember that our God is mighty. He is strong. He loves you and wants to see you succeed. Don't feel like you have to digest this entire book at one time. If you aren't walking at this time in the freedom that you desire, keep at it. God doesn't care about how long it takes you to succeed. He just cares that you are trying. I am still growing and learning, and I am confident that you will find the freedom you desire also.

My prayer for you can be found in the words of Paul in Philippians 1:3–6:

> I thank my God upon every remembrance of you, always in every prayer of mine making request for you all with joy, for your fellowship in the gospel from the first day until now, being confident of this very thing, that *He who has begun a good work in you will complete it until the day of Jesus Christ.* (emphasis my own)

Be encouraged. Keep your eyes on Christ. Hebrews 12:2 says to "fix our eyes on Jesus, the author and perfecter of our faith, who for the joy set before Him endured the cross, scorning its shame, and sat down at the right hand of the throne of God." Look to Him for your healing. Look to Him for your faith.

From this point forward, I am confident that God is going to complete that good work in you. Why? Because I think that if you were willing to spend all of this time with me, you are taking seriously the words of Paul in Philippians 3:14. He says:

> Brethren, I do not count myself to have apprehended; but one thing I do, forgetting those things which are behind and reaching forward to those things which are ahead, I press toward the goal for the prize of the upward call of God in Christ Jesus.
>
> —NLT

Press on. Keep moving toward your goal of freedom. Keep Christ always in front of you, and I promise you, He will meet you at the finish line with a towel, a cool drink, and a hug to say, "Well done."

Be blessed. Keep walking in victory. I would love to hear from you. Visit me on the web at www.thesearchforfreedom. org.

In Christ,
Garrett Drew Ellis

APPENDICES

FOUND BY GOD: GARRETT DREW ELLIS' STORY

I love these words:

> For I am persuaded that neither death nor life, nor angels nor principalities nor powers, nor things present nor things to come, nor height nor depth, nor any other created thing, shall be able to separate us from the love of God which is in Christ Jesus our Lord.
>
> —Romans 8:38–39

I DIDN'T ALWAYS KNOW that these words were written in the Bible, but for as long as I can remember, I had always thought that if there was a God, there was no way that He could ever love me. I was too messed up. I had been hurt and had caused hurt in too many situations. Even though this was my way of thinking for so long, I would eventually come to know and cherish these words because God showed me firsthand that they were true in a very real way.

Prior to coming to know God, I had always struggled with same sex attractions. Since the time I was a young child I knew that I had attractions for boys and men but never knew why I could not find comfort in those feelings . I never could be happy with them, despite the encouragement I received from well-intentioned friends, family, and general members of society to accept it and be happy. Although a father who loved me more than the moon and the stars raised me to believe in my own self worth, I had none. I always felt that my inability to love myself kept me bound. So I struggled very hard for over thirteen years with my sexuality, living a hidden life and hating myself the entire time. I tried to commit suicide twice because of my inability to line up my feelings about my sexuality with the things that I wanted out of life.

It was not until college that I found any true freedom from any of these feelings. I was in the grip of major depression and on the verge of becoming suicidal once again when some people came into my life that helped me to change it forever.

The Road to God

The first person was a girl I met on campus. Because I felt like I had to hide the other side of my sexuality, I began a relationship with her. I was truly attracted to her both physically and emotionally, but part of my motivation for approaching her was to strengthen the façade I had covering my complete heterosexuality. The thing I did not realize was that she saw past all of that and went into the relationship with the gut feeling that I was attracted to men. She looked past my faults and was able to see my needs, namely, someone to show me that I was worth being loved.

The second person who came into my life was the girl's grandmother. During the summer months between semesters, the girl took me home to meet her family. It was at this time that her grandmother took one look at me upon our first meeting and did nothing more for a little over an hour than tell me about how much God loved the world, how He was able to change any negative thing in our lives to something positive, and how He is holy and wants us to be holy, too. Without ever mentioning one word or opinion about my sexuality, she told me that God loved me more than I could ever imagine and that He wanted me to come to know Him, to be obedient to the way He wants me to live so that I could experience life abundantly.

I thought she was crazy. I had never heard anything like this before. I had been to church occasionally when I was young, but I thought church life was about attending every once in awhile, listening to the choir, and then heading back to the real world. I knew nothing about a God who was involved in our daily lives, a God who wanted us to be better than what we were. I thought that was what psychologists were for.

So I went on with life, thinking that I had simply heard the ramblings of a crazy, old lady. But here's the crazy thing. Even though I continued to deal with the depression on my own, I never forgot her words. For the major part of a year, they wouldn't leave the back of my mind. The thought that God could possibly help me to change my sexual feelings for men was totally new and refreshing.

In the upcoming months, life got hectic. This girl and I began to connect on a very spiritual level. We had so much in common that we began to depend on each other, not only for sex, but also for everything. Eventually, we fell in love. But I knew that we couldn't go into a real relationship without her knowing about my past. And if she knew about my past, I would have to take the chance of her leaving. And at this point, I didn't want her to. I loved her.

But it just so happened that after the fall semester started, she came back to campus from a weekend trip a different person. She was talking about God and how He had "saved" her. She was saying that He had changed her heart because she had given her heart to Him. And to put the icing on the cake, she said that sex was no longer going to be a part of our relationship.

The crazy woman must have gotten to her.

So we went back and forth a couple of weeks, debating the spiritual significance of God. I couldn't seem to accept the idea of His existence, but I also couldn't seem to get away from two things. One, the idea that He could possibly help me to overcome my feelings for men and two, that despite the end of our sexual relationship, this girl and I were becoming closer and closer, more bonded together than I could possibly have imagined.

The night I met Him

The night I came to know God was a weird one. It was a night kind of like any other night, except that I was extremely nervous. We were at the girl, Dayona's, mom's house, and I had decided that this was the night I was going to have to spill the beans, because I was tired of carrying it around on my chest. I didn't know how God was going to fit into the equation, but I knew that if she and I were going to move forward, she was going to have to know.

We were watching movies or something, and I got up from the couch and walked into the kitchen. I stood by the sink with this empty feeling in the pit of my stomach. I couldn't sit still, and I knew that she suspected I was about to hit her with something because she kept glancing at me from the corner of her eye. Eventually she went upstairs to the bathroom or something, and I sat back down on the couch. When I get nervous, I get aggravated—eventually I let out a string of curses and decided that I needed to stop being a punk and just do it. So I called out her name and asked her to come back downstairs.

The TV was still playing, but when she came down (in her pajamas), I asked her to sit next to me, and I kind of blocked out everything around me. She was really quiet and just stared at me. I told her that I needed to say something to her but didn't know how. She told me to go ahead, and even though I had rehearsed this big speech over and over in my head, the only two words I could find were: "I'm gay." I don't know why, but before I actually said them, I started crying. Tears were running down my face, almost on the verge of big, gigantic sobs. I got the words out even though they were really choppy and almost unrecognizable. I must have said it two or three times, and by the third time, I was crying so hard that they were hard to understand.

Now this is the part that is blurry and hard to understand. I know now that everyone's conversion experience isn't an emotional one, but mine was. From the minute I spoke the words "I'm gay," I don't remember the room, I don't remember Dayona sitting next to me, and I don't remember anything except a lot of emptiness. I don't know how to describe it, but for a time, I felt very much alone—like the world was shapeless, empty, and filled to the brim with absolutely nothing. And it was at this time that I spoke to God for the first time. I don't know why I did. I just did. I felt like He was the only one in the room, so if I was going to tell anyone all of this, it was going to have to be Him.

Words began to flow out of my mouth, words that spoke of how sorry I was, how utterly sorry I was, that I had done all that I had done. I have never been one to raise my voice before, but in those moments, I needed God to hear me loud and clear because I was very much alone and by myself. I could not depend on anyone to relay the message for me, because no one was there. I didn't know the name "Jesus," and I didn't know about the cross or Calvary or about blood or any of those things; all I knew in that moment was that if there was a God out there, I needed Him very badly because I had messed up royally. I needed Him so badly that I was finally willing to do whatever it took to fill up that world with something or someone that was able to forgive me for all the sex, lies, betrayals, hurts, and pain. I needed something real that was able to tell me that I was worth something and that it really, really loved me and that if I wanted it to, it would be there to change me into something better—or at the very least, into someone who felt less pain and less loneliness.

This went on for hours. I must have been crying and carrying on for a long time because it was very late when I came around. But when I did, I saw the most beautiful sight in the world. I saw Dayona sitting on the couch, still in her pajamas, still listening and praying and crying with me. She didn't look any different, she had not changed in any way. But the simple fact that she had listened in on this conversation that I had had with God and was still there made her look different, look better, more like the something I needed more than anything else. She sat through a conversation that spoke of the type of sex I had had, the men I had been with, and the lies I had told, and still she was there, without a disgusted look on her face or even a hint of anger.

When I finally got myself together, I knew I was different. Or at least, I would never be what I was before the void. I still didn't know exactly what had happened or what was going on, but I knew that there was substance where there was none before. There was something that wasn't there before moving around in me, moving in that void and that space of nothing. And the one who helped usher it in was sitting next to me on the couch.

Then it hit me. The crazy, old lady! Dayona's crazy grandmother! Was this the God she was talking about? It must have been, because Dayona was sitting next to me, still claiming to know Him and telling me that everything she had heard me tell Him was everything that He had wanted to hear. She told me that her grandmother had preached Him to her and that now she was going to preach Him to me. She said that I needed to accept Him into my life because He wanted to do everything that I had asked Him to do. She said that if I would open my eyes I'd see that He had already begun that work, because she was still there, not going anywhere.

So I accepted Jesus as my Savior. Just like that. After that type of experience, I felt like I had to give Him a chance. What else, who else, besides God could make this girl stay with a guy who had just admitted he liked men? Who else offered me the possibility to change? It was at that moment that I gave God my life and free rein to do whatever He must in order to bring me closer to Him and to her.

Do you see why I value this woman so much? She never has been and never will be my object of worship or my god, but she was so instrumental, so extremely important in my coming to know Christ, that it astounds me how she sometimes doesn't realize the level of connectedness we have, regardless of how I needed to learn to change how I was intimate with another person. She was His instrument of grace when I needed it the most. He knew that in those moments, at that time when I would feel the most forsaken, forgotten, and alone, I would need something to touch and see that would look and act and treat me exactly as He would if I were able to see Him physically. He knew I couldn't do that, so He took Dayona and used her to be not only the gift of a future wife but also His representative the first time He wanted to chat with me.

I forgot to say that this all happened in the wee hours of Dayona's twentieth birthday. I had encountered God on the day that she was born, and I, too, felt like it was my own day to come into the world. I left the house in the morning in search of a birthday gift for her, but everywhere I went, my eyes hurt with the newness of everything around me. The sky was so much bigger, the light was so much brighter, the world seemed so much fuller, like spaces had been filled in and filled up with things that were not there before. It was a day unlike any other and a day unlike any I have seen since.

Eventually, we began going to church and meeting with other Christians on campus. I learned that the God I met that night was Jesus. I learned the theological explanation for what had happened in terms of being born again. I learned about what it was that I had been searching for, the explanation in its fullness, wrapped up in what it meant to be a Christian.

These things were all well and good, necessary and valuable to know, but I will never forget the day I met Him, when no one or nothing else was around, the day it was just Him, me, and the woman I can call my friend.

The crazy old lady died the following February. Even though I had only known her for a very short amount of time, I will always remember the fact that she planted the seed of God in my life.

I learned later that God saved me. When I use the word "saved," I mean it in a couple of ways. First, I am referencing the Bible, where, in Romans chapter 10, Paul tells us, "If you would confess with your mouth the Lord Jesus and believe in your heart that God has raised Him from the dead, you will be saved." I had never been given the option of being able to live a happy heterosexual life except by the preaching of the gospel that I heard from sincere Christians like Dayona, her grandmother, and Christians on campus. I chose to believe in the tenets of Christianity and thus began the process of being "saved" from a guilty sentence in the eyes of God. I also began continually bringing my daily shortcomings to Him so that He could forgive and help me to change the way I lived.

Secondly, when I say "saved," I mean that this belief in Christ literally saved my life. I was on a path of deep depression, was suicidal in many ways, and was destructive in my behavior in order to find same sex intimacy. I did not know that God had a way of allowing me to meet my need to be accepted by men without using sex to do so. This came through affirmation of my manhood and identity in Christ through godly men.

Even after all of this, I still had struggles, and I still experienced temptation, but from the point of my conversion, I found that I had the power to control my actions and reactions. Now when I fell, it was because I was not taking the way of escape from temptation that God always offers. The Bible says, "No temptation has seized you except what is common to man. And God is faithful; he will not let you be tempted beyond what you can bear. But when you are tempted, he will also provide a way out so that you can stand up under it" (1 Cor. 10:13 NIV). The way of escape is always there—we just have to use it.

Before becoming a Christian, I thought that I would probably have to live my life alone, not wanting a man and not being able to find a woman who would love me the way I was. I thought that I would never have kids and the family that I desired. But I was wrong. Even though I know that it doesn't happen to every struggling man the way it happened for me, Dayona and I are now happily married and have three children. God gives abundantly more than we can ask or think when we learn to love Him.

Now, life isn't perfect. There came a time in our marriage when sin tried to reenter my life. At this point, because of some weaknesses of my own and unchecked motives, I committed adultery with a man. I fell again into a very deep depression and almost allowed my marriage to fail because of it. But two things happened that put me back on the road to serving God.

The first thing, once again, happened to be Dayona. During this time of intense pain, God saw fit to talk to her, giving her the strength, patience, and love necessary to remain married to me. She put aside her own feelings of hurt and shame and told me that we were in this fight together. I was battling against a lifestyle that wasn't compatible with God, and she was in the battle with me. She took on the fight against my attractions with renewed vigor, vowing to remain with me not only as a wife and friend, but also as a sister in Christ as long as I was willing to recommit myself to God.

The second thing that happened was that the Lord saw fit to allow a man to come into my life and gave me a friendship that has been the epitome of healthy, Christian love. I have a father and older brother whom I love and respect highly, but I never had a committed Christian friend to show me what manhood looks like. It was through this mentor that I began to really strengthen my walk with God, learning what it means to be a man in His eyes. This mentor has discipled me, opened me up to the Word of God, and shown me an example of manhood that is beyond comparison. It was through this man and his wife that my wife and I found counsel to strengthen and renew our marriage. It was also through this couple that we were able to relocate our family to an area that was better suited for our growth. For this, I am truly grateful to God.

Through all of this and even the struggles that I as an individual and we as a couple face today, we have learned that the Lord is truly the Director and Guide in our lives and that the grace of God to reconcile, renew, and equip is truly astounding. I am committed to allowing the Lord to reign fully in my life and the lives of my family through worship and service. My testimony of overcoming and walking in the freedom of the Lord is simply a witness of the power that He holds and testifies that He truly is the liberator of those that want freedom. The crux of the issue lies in the fact who freedom must be desired. An opening of the heart or willingness to give God a chance to be God must be established.

God in His infinite love saw that we were not living according to or meeting up with the standard of how He would have us live our lives. But this did not stop Him. While someone who did not love us would have left us to the die in the wilderness, God sent a very special part of Himself to *die* for us, even when we were not willing to acknowledge Him (Romans 5:8).

God sees our separation from Him as being worthy of death. That separation is shown when we are disobedient to the lifestyle and purpose He has called us to. But His love is just as strong. He sent His Son, Jesus (who was God Himself and would be known as the Christ), to earth to die in our place. This paid the price of death that God the Father needed. We are granted fellowship with God if we will submit to living as Christ lived. This includes believing that God raised Him from the dead to pay for and overcome our sins. This faith in Christ restores our relationship to God and grants us eternal life in His coming kingdom. On top of these gifts, He grants us the power, through Christ, to overcome the addictions, contrary lifestyles, habits, and spirits of disobedience that can separate us from His fellowship.

He did this for me. I am confident of my place in heaven and am glad to say that I am able to overcome the homosexual lifestyle that I didn't want. But without this faith, we will pay the price of death ourselves and be separated from Him forever.

I believe that He is willing and able to do the same thing for you. Believe in Him today. Give Him your heart, mind, soul, and strength. He says, "If you confess with your mouth the Lord Jesus and believe in your heart that God has raised Him from the dead, you will be saved" (Romans 10:9).

I didn't understand that His love is limitless. I didn't understand that simply asking Him to do something and believing in the things He has done opens up the doorway to His pouring out bucket loads of adoration on us. Please don't live life without His love working in your life the way I did for so long. He loves you. Love Him back today.

RESOURCES FOR GROWTH

But grow in the grace and knowledge of our Lord and
Savior Jesus Christ. To Him be the glory both now and
forever. Amen.

—2 Peter 3:18

HERE ARE SOME resources for your continued
growth. They include ministries for men journeying out of homosexuality and books on the
same topic.They also include tools on general Christian
principles. Through all of these, you will also find other
resources that will promote your freedom and keep you
looking to Jesus, the Author and Finisher of your faith.

Ministries

- www.thesearchforfreedom.org: Our website is
  designed as a place of encouragement, fellowship,
  and information for you as we walk on this journey

towards freedom from homosexuality. On it you can find a mentorship program, Bible study aids, links to upcoming and established ministries, and a blog where I write about the topic of freedom from homosexuality.

- www.exodus-international.org: Exodus International is the oldest ex-gay referral ministry in the world. Its website is designed to point you towards online resources, local support groups and ministries, as well as a plethora of books, articles, and information.

Books

This is a list of books that have blessed me and allowed me to continue moving forward in freedom. It includes books on the topic of freedom from homosexuality as well as other topics (devotionals, Bible studies, and literature). It is by no means exhaustive. The first source, hands down, is the Bible, both the Old and New Testaments. I often use the New International Version, the New King James Version, and the New Living Translation, but these are just suggestions.

On Sexual Purity and Freedom from Homosexuality

- *Growth into Manhood* by Alan Medinger
- *Straight and Narrow?* by Thomas E. Schmidt
- *Pursuing Sexual Wholeness* by Andrew Comiskey
- *Out of the Depths of Sexual Sin* by Steve Gallagher

Devotional or General Christian inspiration

- *The Purpose Driven Life* by Rick Warren
- *The Case for Christ* by Lee Strobel
- *My Utmost for His Highest* by Oswald Chambers
- *Battlefield of the Mind* by Joyce Meyer
- *The Life You've Always Wanted* by John Ortberg
- *The Pilgrim's Progress* by John Bunyan (Try to find a modern language version.)
- *The Screwtape Letters, Mere Christianity,* and *The Chronicles of Narnia* by C.S. Lewis
- *The Unquenchable Worshipper* by Matt Redman

Internet Filtering System

www.safeeyes.com: This is probably the best Internet filtering system available today. Check it out.

APPENDIX C

SCRIPTURE MEMORIZATION

THROUGHOUT THIS BOOK, I have tried to stress the importance of memorizing Scripture. It doesn't make you holier or cleaner, but it does allow you to have the Word of God always at your access for fighting temptation, delighting in God, and getting closer to Him.

Listed here are the memory verses from each section. What I want you to do is go out and buy a pack of index cards. Write out each of the verses and begin the practice of carrying these around with you on a daily basis.

In the western world, we are blessed to have an abundance of English translations of the Bible available to us, but carrying a Bible around with us everywhere we go is not always a possibility. These cards are an easy way of having a small, compact piece of the Word with us at all times. As you begin to commit these verses to memory, make new cards with other verses. Also, feel free to add the other

Scripture references from any of the sections in this book to the following list.

- 1 Corinthians 6:9–10
- John 3:17
- John 15:9
- Jude 24
- Revelation 3:20
- 2 Corinthians 3:17
- 1 Peter 5:8–9
- 1 Corinthians 10:3–5
- Luke 15:10, 24
- 2 Corinthians 5:17
- Psalm 51:7, 9
- Matthew 17:21
- Romans 13:14
- Proverbs 27:17
- Genesis 2:18, 24

ENDNOTES

1. Lacey, Rob, *The Word on the Street*, Zondervan, 2003, Grand Rapids, MI
2. Ortberg, John, *The Life You've Always Wanted*, Zondervan, 2002, Grand Rapids, MI
3. Towns, Elmer *Fasting for Spiritual Breakthrough*, Regal Books, 1996, Ventura, CA

PW

Breinigsville, PA USA
20 May 2010
238435BV00001B/111/P